THE

COURAGEOUS

LEADER

HOW TO FACE ANY CHALLENGE AND LEAD YOUR TEAM TO *SUCCESS*

ANGELA SEBALY

WILEY

Published by John Wiley & Sons, Inc., Hoboken, New Jersey.
Published simultaneously in Canada.

Library of Congress Cataloging-in-Publication Data:

Names: Sebaly, Angela, author.
Title: The courageous leader : how to face any challenge and lead your team
    to success / Angela Sebaly.
Description: Hoboken : Wiley, 2017. | Includes bibliographical references and
    index.
Identifiers: LCCN 2016054685 (print) | LCCN 2016055857 (ebook) | ISBN
    9781119331612 (hardback) | ISBN 9781119331803 (Adobe PDF) | ISBN
    9781119331810 (ePub)
Subjects: LCSH: Leadership. | Success in business. | BISAC: BUSINESS &
    ECONOMICS / Leadership.
Classification: LCC HD57.7 .S4287 2017 (print) | LCC HD57.7 (ebook) | DDC
    658.4/092–dc23
LC record available at https://lccn.loc.gov/2016054685

Printed in the United States of America

10 9 8 7 6 5 4 3 2 1

Dedication

To my daughter, Cate, the most courageous soul I know.

CONTENTS

FOREWORD

I've known Angela Sebaly for nearly a decade, first as a client and now as my business partner at Personify Leadership. For as long as I have known her, she has always modeled courage. From coaching CEOs of Fortune 500 companies to taking a leap of faith starting a new business, Angela is not one to back down from a challenge. One trait that I admire in Angela is that she has the innate ability to sense a problem early and will address it without hesitation. She has the courage to say the tough stuff, often eliminating a problem before it becomes one. She demands excellence from others because she first requires it of herself—that in itself takes a lot of courage. Angela's fervent commitment to addressing the tough stuff early makes her not only courageous but also a leader who is continuing to grow herself. She is thoughtful, strategic, and results driven.

What qualifies Angela Sebaly to write this book is that she lives as a courageous leader every day. She is one of the most talented coaches I know. She can challenge leaders to unpack what's really going on and then help them make small behavioral changes in a thoughtful and effective way. Her ability to role model courage inspires me to have more courageous conversations. When I am mentally preparing for a courageous conversation, I will often ask myself, "How would Angela address this? What questions might Angela ask?" Even when those courageous conversations I must have are *with* Angela, I still find myself thinking about how she would be talking to me, if the situation were reversed.

Throughout the pages of this book, Angela shares lessons from leaders she has coached and worked with, as well as the lessons she has personally learned—and continues to learn—about courageous leadership. Drawing upon her varied life experiences, she flushes out vital principles and riveting firsthand stories. This is far more than another book on leadership lessons. You will walk away with true strategies and techniques to be a more courageous leader.

Michelle Cummings, coauthor of
A Teachable Moment and
author of *Setting the Conflict Compass*

INTRODUCTION

Consider the role courageous leaders play in our society—from the firefighter who runs into a burning building to the feminist who challenges conventional thinking to the athlete who pushes physical boundaries. We are inspired by them, we learn from them, and we are protected by them. *Now, imagine a world without them.*

During the Revolutionary War, two sailors named Samuel Shaw and Richard Marven witnessed their leader, the commander of the Continental Navy, participating in the torture of captured British sailors. The sailors knew what they were up against with Commodore Esek Hopkins. He came from a powerful family and was in a position of power in a newly formed government. It was risky to say or do anything to stop Hopkins, but both Shaw and Marven believed that it was their duty to report their superior's misconduct. In 1777, their worst fears were realized when they were arrested after Hopkins retaliated by filing a libel suit against them. However, later that same month, Congress enacted the first whistle-blower act and not only released the two men but also agreed to pay their attorneys' fees.[1]

Imagine a world without Shaw and Marven.

Fast-forward to more than a century later when an outbreak of the Ebola virus in western Africa killed more than 11,000 people and became the most deadly and feared virus on the planet. The doctors, nurses, and caregivers working with the Ebola virus became our saviors. While many medical staff, understandably, resigned on the spot, others went into hospitals and makeshift treatment facilities armed with their medical training, and more important, their concern for human life and their indisputable courage.[2]

Just out of school, completing his medical internship, Dr. Jerry Brown was hardly prepared for leading the fight against Ebola, but he faced his patients anyway, looking them in the eye as he diagnosed them and cared for them. In Liberia, his hospital filled quickly with infected patients but with a limited number of staff willing to take their chances. Brown told a group of students at the Case Western Reserve University School of Medicine, "The first thought that I had was, 'If we do nothing, this disease is going to overrun us, and before you get to know it, there won't be any country called Liberia.'" Brown said, "We had to do something. We couldn't run away."[3]

Imagine a world without Dr. Jerry Brown and the caretakers of Ebola patients.

Halfway across the world on a train to Paris in late August of 2015, five men—a British businessman, two American military men, one American tourist, and a Frenchman—were about to become heroes. The hum of their otherwise average day was interrupted by the sound of a gunshot and shattered glass. An unknown man entered their train car with an AK-47 assault rifle.

The five men jumped into action, tackling the attacker, then hog-tying him and holding him down until the train could stop and the French police could take him into custody. All the while, other passengers stood in shock, horror, and disbelief, considering the incredible tragedy that was averted by the swift and selfless acts of these five men.

Later, French president François Hollande said the men showed us "that faced with terror, we have the power to resist. They also gave us a lesson in courage, in will, and thus, in hope."[4]

Imagine a world without five heroes on a train.

Courage is what moves us to action in the face of tough times. Without it, we suffer from our humanity instead of rising above it.

The good news is that courage is accessible to everyone. It is not in short supply or limited to the elite, powerful, rich, or heavily trained. It is something we all have the capacity to obtain once we understand the origin of it and how to overcome the obstacles to leveraging it.

Courage Is the Way

Although the demographic makeup of leaders varies dramatically, their challenges largely remain the same. Leaders of all shapes and sizes are asked to make tough decisions, have tough conversations, take on tough workloads, inspire tough people, and achieve tough goals. These challenges are not unique. But not all leaders are capable of doing the tough stuff. What separates a good manager from an exceptional leader is the willingness to face any challenge rather than avoid it, delegate it, or run from it. Simply put, when the time comes, does the leader have the courage to move to action?

Best-selling author Elizabeth Gilbert found her resolve to continue writing after six years of being rejected because, as she explained, "I loved writing more than I hated failing at writing."[5] Maybe one of the key questions you have to answer for yourself to be a courageous leader is this: *Do you love leading more than you hate failing at it?*

Let me be the first to provide you some leadership absolutes if you haven't already figured them out for yourself. You *will* fail. You *will* fall down and scrape your knees, break a bone, and maybe even end up in a body cast (metaphorically speaking, of course). There *will* be pain. Courage is the willingness to do something in the face of fear, discomfort, and pain. As a result, courage is what separates those of us who want something from those of us who actually achieve it.

Individuals enter into leadership for their own reasons. Some find themselves there by accident, and others have simply been anointed leader without any real understanding of what it means, often emulating behaviors of old bosses, both good and bad. Some decide to become leaders because of the paycheck or because of the image their ego conjures up about the status and power leadership brings. In these cases, the ego is the leader's oxygen, and like a diver without a tank, he or she eventually suffocates. Rarely do individuals enter into leadership with the intention to serve others or something bigger than themselves—even though it's what gets results long term. The kind of selflessness that goes along with this kind of leadership, as you will learn, is challenging and requires courage.

Courageous leadership is a choice. In each of us, a seed of possibility exists as our potential state. Standing at the crossroads of reality and dreams, it is those who are courageous who ultimately find their way to achieving their goals. There are no hidden roadblocks intentionally set out to derail success or make leaders struggle unnecessarily. The path to courageous leadership is as different as our DNA, but it is equally accessible to everyone.

The Three Components of Courage: Diversity, Pain, and Choice

So where do we start? If courage is equally accessible, then why don't we all leverage courage equally? What gets in the way?

Often what limits us from leveraging courage is our own preconceived notions about it. We see courage as a muscle that we either have or don't. Those of us lucky enough to have it can use it while the rest of us have to resort to lesser, more available tools. Yet every human is equipped with approximately 300 unique muscles to stretch, strengthen, and leverage. When we underestimate the diversity of courage, we also underestimate the possibility it brings. There are many ways to see courage and to access it. For a firefighter, courage is stepping into a burning building, but for a schoolteacher, courage may be addressing with a parent unproductive behaviors at home that lead to class dysfunction.

Embracing the diversity of courage is just one part. Pain and choice are equally as important. Just like in our bodies, when we first start using our muscles, we feel pain. Anyone who's joined a gym for the first time as a New Year's resolution knows this well. Your first day is full of promise and excitement. Dressed in your workout gear pulled from a box in your closet, you enter the gym with your favorite music blaring on your iPhone only to find that after just 20 minutes of exercise, your chest hurts, you can barely breathe, and you're ready to pass out. And that's not the best part. Two days later, the lactic acid in your muscles has built up, and you can't seem to remember how to walk or move without excruciating pain. It's no surprise, then, that there is a high attrition rate of people who give up their gym memberships by March.

Pain will follow the act of building courage just as it does building a muscle. We can accept that pain either as our body's white flag of surrender or as feedback that we are making necessary progress. It's up to us to decide. Make no mistake—it is a choice.

Therefore, to build a complete courage toolbox, we'll need to explore the diversity of courage, embrace pain as part of the process, and make the choice to engage courage fully. To do this, in *The Courageous Leader*, we'll look at courage in a multifaceted way:

The Courage to Get Unstuck. "The Courage to Get Unstuck" challenges you to consider that discomfort or pain may be an indication you are stuck. Oftentimes, we find ourselves stuck when we are unwilling to move past the fear of making a needed change that would otherwise propel us forward professionally.

The Courage to Take a Stand. "The Courage to Take a Stand" is about identifying what is important to you. In this chapter, you'll evaluate your own values and priorities so that your courageous decisions and actions are aligned with who you are and what you believe is right for you and your organization.

The Courage to Be Humble. "The Courage to Be Humble" introduces the power of humility as a tool for leadership growth.

Specifically, we'll introduce The Humbling Experience and the importance of courage to get back up after you have been brought to your knees.

The Courage to Be Confident. "The Courage to Be Confident" looks at the opposite of arrogance and encourages the development of self-confidence and self-trust in leadership, while identifying the consequences when you don't exemplify this courage.

The Courage to Delegate. "The Courage to Delegate" is a window into the struggles leaders face when delegating, and more important, the struggles they face when they don't delegate. In some ways, delegation is one of the most vulnerable things a leader can do, and in that vulnerability, there are risk, fear, and pain that require courage.

The Courage to Give and Receive Feedback. "The Courage to Give and Receive Feedback" illuminates the importance of having tough conversations in the midst of tough times for clarifying meaning, as well as obtaining healthy results long term.

The Courage to Be in the Middle. "The Courage to Be in the Middle" takes a deep dive into the world of systems thinking, specifically the work of Barry Oshry and the courage it takes to live in the middle space of organizational life.

Grow, Recover, Repeat. In the first eight chapters, you'll explore ways in which you need to push past the pain and do the right thing for your team's and organization's success as part of their growth. That kind of courage is exhausting and requires appropriate recovery to continue to maintain a courageous approach to leadership. In this chapter, you will explore methods of recovery after growth.

Big Dreams, Big Moves. In all of us is the ability to soar beyond our wildest imaginations, but we mostly don't. It's not that it is out of our control to live up to our potential but that we haven't challenged ourselves enough to live our Big Dreams by making

Big Moves toward those dreams. This chapter serves as the conduit to begin moving from possibility to planned success and measurable outcomes.

The Intention of the Author and This Book

Over the course of 20 years, I have worked with leaders all over the world, from varying backgrounds, levels of expertise, and industries. I've worked as their peer, their coach, their facilitator, their teacher, and their guide. I've had the great privilege of observing their courageous stories unfold, one leader at a time. They may not have considered themselves courageous, but I do. Even those who failed, or at least failed in the moment I was with them on their journey, demonstrated great courage in their willingness to suit up and play the game. I am the keeper of their stories. I have an endless bookshelf built in my mind that holds their triumphs and their misfortunes. I hope that, as I share these stories with you, you will also gain a significant appreciation for the role courage plays in leadership. Although there is no magic formula to being courageous, I'll share with you *my* formula for courage, concocted from the study of experiences.

Because learning can be vulnerable, it is important to me, as I assimilate the experiences of the leaders I've worked with into telling the story of *The Courageous Leader*, that I reflect as much of their real experiences as possible, while maintaining their confidentiality. In most cases, I've changed the leaders' names. In others, where the details of a story point more clearly to a person and situation, I've altered the details while honoring the intent of the stories as much as possible. Some stories I tell represent a collective story of many leaders told as one to convey the purpose of their learning; these stories are not factually based on any one person or situation.

It is also important to communicate that, at times, I share leaders' stories as they conveyed them to me during an interview. At other times, I tell the stories from my own perspective, observations, and point of view. I am an expert in leadership development, but to say that the assessment and conclusions I draw from their experiences is the definitive way to view the situation is contrary to the goal of this book. Instead, I hope that as I share my perspective, it not only illuminates possibilities but also provides space for readers to filter the insight through their own lens and absorb it as they see fit.

In addition to telling the stories of leaders, I also share my personal stories as an everyday leader struggling to grow a business, raise a family, and give back to my community. Just wait until you read some of *my* humbling experiences! I find I'm often just one fall and rise up ahead of many of the leaders I lead. The warning signs and strategies are almost obvious in hindsight but often feel invisible when you need them most. As a result, I'm always eager—after brushing myself off and regaining my composure—to share what I learn from personal experiences. Those who have agreed to share their real stories feel the same.

Regardless of my methodology in storytelling, my intent is to create empathy and understanding, to normalize the fact that leadership is hard stuff, and to provide the reader with insight and tools for how to be a leader who is courageous in tough times.

It is my hope that sharing stories of courageous leadership will inspire you to think about what else is possible for you. You are not alone. Your struggles are synonymous with leadership, regardless of your title. *CEO* does not stand for *superhero*. Despite your trail of rich successes or mountain of intense failures, this book was written to be a guide.

Each chapter will outline stories and strategies for living courageously as a leader. At the end of each chapter, you'll see a section called "Chapter Application," where you'll be provided questions to consider that will help you apply what you've learned in the book to your real-world experiences. If the chapter doesn't already provide strategies for developing the specific skills introduced in the chapter, you'll also see a section for strategies to practice.

I ask that, as you begin this book, you give yourself permission to be a learner and stay open to the possibility that you will take away exactly what you need from the time you invest in it.

Notes

1. Cohn, Stephen M. "The Whistle-Blowers of 1777." *New York Times*, June 12, 2011. http://www.nytimes.com/2011/06/13/opinion/13kohn.html?_r=0.

2. von Drehle, David. "The Ebola Fighters: The Ones Who Answered the Call." With Aryn Baker. *Time*, December 10, 2014. http://time.com/time-person-of-the-year-ebola-fighters/.

3. Ross, Casey. "Ebola Fighter Dr. Jerry Brown Tells Story of Courage and Hope in Appearance at Case Western." June 12, 2011. http://www.cleveland.com/healthfit/index.ssf/2015/10/ebola_dr_jerry_brown_tells_sto.htmlInsert.

4. Corbet, Sylvie. "Americans, Briton Receive Award from French President." August 24, 2015. https://www.bostonglobe.com/news/world/2015/08/24/americans-briton-gave-lesson-courage-french-president-says/nPveYO5L2jZ-1RnhmBvMqjN/story.html.

5. Gilbert, Elizabeth. "Success, Failure and the Drive to Keep Creating" (TED Talk transcript). April 2014. https://www.ted.com/talks/elizabeth_gilbert_success_failure_and_the_drive_to_keep_creating/transcript?language=en.

1 The Business Case for Courage

Life shrinks or expands in proportion to one's courage.[1]

—Anaïs Nin

Anna is the kind of person we all want to work with. She is considerate, compassionate, and approachable. In an industry where attracting and retaining talent is nearly impossible, Anna has been extraordinarily successful at keeping her people happy. When I first met Anna, I was in the process of visiting various locations throughout her organization to facilitate feedback from employees in the field. Before meeting Anna and her team, I had heard nothing but gripes from overworked and underpaid employees in other locations, most of whom pointed their fingers at poor leadership—especially in the "disconnected" corporate office. But Anna's team offered a very different perspective. Their unique account of their experiences was uplifting. I spoke with one team member who held one of the least desirable jobs in the company, having to work at all hours of the night to dispatch calls from employees in the field. He said, "Even if the competition paid me double, I wouldn't leave this company. Anna treats us like family."

Anna did, in fact, strike me as a warm and caring matriarch, protectively hovering and providing for her flock. My visit fell on a Friday morning, and per tradition, Anna had brought in her homemade pastries. Before she could set them down on the breakroom table, greedy hands dug in, and her team clustered together to catch up on the week. I used this time as an opportunity to informally learn more about Anna's leadership. I heard nothing but praise for Anna's kindness and generosity.

After such an unusual visit, I returned to the corporate office to report back to the divisional president, excited to share a success story amid the myriad of dysfunctional stories I had cataloged during previous site visits. When I concluded sharing my testimonial to Anna's great leadership, the president shook his head in disappointment. He then pulled up an Excel spreadsheet and began walking me through Anna's key performance indicators compared to her peers in similar positions around the country.

On average, Anna paid her employees 25 percent more than other teams, even though the cost of living in her region was significantly less expensive. She had three times more resources allocated to the team's workload than her counterparts, and yet her branch was underperforming in every metric the company measured. In fact, year after year, the problems had progressively gotten worse. The president said, "Anna's people are happy and they don't leave because she babies them and lets them get away with not working. She doesn't do the hard stuff, and she is failing." He continued, "If she really cared about her people, she'd make some tough decisions because as it stands now, her branch is in jeopardy of being eliminated altogether." Six months later, Anna and her 60 employees were let go, and her office was closed.

Throughout the world, a business's success ultimately hinges on two things: the ability to increase revenue and the ability to drive down costs. Even if the business is a nonprofit whose mission is to save lives, without donations coming in and cost being managed, the mission cannot be achieved. In an ever increasingly competitive marketplace of doing more with less, it's not what you did for me yesterday that matters but what you can do for me today. Shareholders want to see progress, customers want innovations, end users want enhancements, and patients want cures. These lofty goals don't manifest themselves. They require risk, overcoming obstacles, facing fears, and challenging the status quo. They require a courageous leader.

The Fear of Discomfort and Pain

When you were growing up, if you were lucky, you may have had one or more parents who said you could be anything you wanted to be—if you just wanted it badly enough and worked hard enough. But desire and work ethic alone are not enough. Courage is a fundamental building block to success. It is what differentiates the dreamers from the achievers. When we think of courageous people, we often associate their courage with their behaviors. And although how we see courage is in action, we often miss an inherent and important step that comes first—our emotions.

To explore this further, consider how you would feel encountering three possible scenarios for yourself. In each of these scenarios, take note of your emotions.

Scenario 1. You just ran into your college roommate for the first time in many years. Imagine for a moment how this encounter would likely play out. Would you be excited to see each other, spilling into old stories about fall homecoming games and late nights studying at the local café? Or would you be embarrassed and ashamed, his or her presence a reminder of how foolish and young you once were? In either case, you likely would feel something. Would you categorize that encounter as pleasant or painful?

Scenario 2. Imagine you are meeting a coworker in the cafeteria the morning following a dispute. You have been concerned that your coworker is unfairly targeting one of your team members and creating unnecessary conflict. On the other hand, he believes you are trying to cover up for your team's poor performance rather than taking responsibility. Your last conversation was heated, and you agreed to disagree.

Now, there he is standing in front of you. How do you feel? Do you imagine this encounter to be pleasant or painful?

Scenario 3. Imagine you are leaving a meeting with your boss during which you both presented to customers. During the presentation, your boss took credit for your ideas and eagerly accepted the praise of the customer. She seems to be oblivious to the problem while you are left baffled. How do you imagine this encounter would likely play out? Would you describe it as pleasant or painful?

The Courageous Leader is about being courageous in tough times. So, what are tough times, and what, exactly, *is* courage?

- Tough times are situations or people we encounter that create some level of discomfort or pain.
- Courage is what moves us to action in the face of tough times.

Recall a time when you were asked to assess your pain on a scale of 1 to 10, with 2 being little pain, 6 moderate pain, and 10 the worst pain you've ever felt. Now, think about the exercise we just completed, considering your emotional responses when you encountered the three different people. What was the level of pain each scenario would have created for you? (Refer to Figure 1.1.)

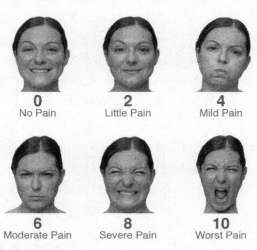

0
No Pain

2
Little Pain

4
Mild Pain

6
Moderate Pain

8
Severe Pain

10
Worst Pain

Figure 1.1 Pain Scale

Most of the time, when we encounter unpleasant people or situations, we experience some level of discomfort and even pain. If you are like most people, confronting your boss about taking credit for your ideas would likely not be comfortable and may even be painful. The fear of that pain is what stalls most leaders. Leaders who lack courage don't have the necessary conversations with their bosses. Instead, they hedge their bets that somehow miraculously the bosses will figure out how they feel and change their behavior accordingly without them having to say or do anything that creates pain. But let's take a step back into Reality Ville for a minute and talk about what really happens. What really happens is that the boss keeps taking credit for work that isn't hers to claim, and the leader puts a lid on the pot of resentment, hoping it doesn't boil over.

After many years of teaching leaders across the globe how to have tough conversations, I noticed one very consistent dilemma arises time and time again. Individuals would leave the class motivated to provide tough feedback to a boss or stand up for themselves to a peer, or talk with a family member about an unresolved dispute. They would also leave armed with new skills, having practiced the conversations competently, and yet nine times out of 10, they would never hold the conversation, or at least not the version they had prepared for. It left me speechless and wondering what was going on. After considering this more carefully, what I've come to understand is that in each of these scenarios, the individuals were both motivated and skilled at facing their tough situation or person head-on, but they lacked the courage to move forward in the face of the pain.

Let's be clear; tough times are more than just tough conversations. Tough times are tough decisions, tough encounters, tough changes, and tough circumstances. The list of scenarios is endless, but here are some examples that commonly show up in the workplace:

- Standing up to the boss about unethical behavior
- Telling an employee he isn't cutting it when he seems to be giving it his all

- Restructuring your organization and eliminating positions
- Getting feedback that others don't believe in you or trust you
- Asking a boss to be more respectful of your time
- Holding someone accountable to his or her commitments
- Disagreeing with your team on an important issue
- Admitting that you made a mistake

Pain Thresholds

Our threshold for pain is entirely subjective. Pain is a stimulus, and how we perceive that stimulus will differ based on our individual propensity to sense it and tolerate it.[2,3] I first became aware of this phenomenon about six months into my first pregnancy. The reality that, to have my baby, I would have to subject myself to a tremendous amount of pain hit me hard. Anyone who knows me understands that, when it comes to physical pain, I am likely to be the first to leave running and screaming. In fact, I passed out the first time I had to get blood drawn and almost hyperventilated when I was informed that drawing blood would be a regular routine until the baby was born. Officially, when it comes to pain, I am a wimp. So the prospect of primal-screaming kind of pain during labor just did not seem like a viable option for me, despite knowing that millions of women—literally—had done this before and survived.

I told my doctor that I wanted to schedule surgery. He seemed a little puzzled, sifting through my file looking for an explanation of my request. When he couldn't find one, he reminded me that I was in good health and so was my baby, and there was no need for surgery. I told him I wanted surgery because I did not like pain. My doctor assured me that there would be pain involved in surgery as well. I asked him whether there would be less pain in surgery than in natural delivery, and he said yes, there would be less pain. When he realized I was serious, he chuckled a little and told me that it was my choice. He said my baby would be healthy and would love me just as much either way. That was all I needed to hear. I left his office with a date for surgery three months later. This, of course, is a decision most moms probably can't fathom and may even shake their heads at in disapproval. And I'm okay with that. I have two healthy children who love me, and I have no knowledge of the pain associated with natural childbirth. I'll accept others' judgment for my ignorance any day. These are consequences I'm willing to accept.

But in leadership, we don't get to cop out so easily. Or if we do, we suffer bigger consequences with larger impact. In leadership, we are responsible for the collective good we represent. When we don't address a problem, we create a dynamic that touches all parts of the system—like a pebble that causes ripples through water. As leaders, our actions do not just affect us alone—ever. Others are watching what we do and listening to what we say, their goal being to observe and determine how we will lead when faced with tough times. Even though our pain tolerances—or thresholds—may differ, with what seems routine for one feeling like walking over hot coals to another, as leaders, we are all held to the same standard. Leaders are expected to be courageous.

Here is the good news. Although courage is not easy, it is accessible to everyone. Here is the not-so-good news. The way to embrace courage is to embrace pain. It's not that courageous leaders derive pleasure from pain but that they are willing to accept pain as part of the process.

Common Reactions to Tough Times

Although our threshold for pain is different, we are likely to have a common reaction to it. Let me illustrate this by sharing a story you can likely relate to. After an incredibly long travel day, I finally landed at my home airport and shuffled my way through the crowds to the walkway to the parking garage. As I stepped off the curb and onto the street, pulling my bag behind me, a large bus was barreling toward me. Without a single thought, I instinctively jumped back onto the curb. It took about 30 seconds before I could process what had just happened. It occurred to me afterward that whatever drew me back to safety was not *me* but something instinctual inside me that sensed danger before my sleepy head could acknowledge it. And that's exactly what happened.

We Feel (We Experience Fear, Discomfort, or Pain)

There is a part of our brain that knows instinctively when danger is imminent. It is called the amygdala. According to the Institute for Health and Human Performance, the amygdala's job is to perceive and respond to threats. It answers the primal question of "Do I eat it or does it eat me?"[4] The amygdala responds to a threat in milliseconds, before the part of our brain that processes information for reasoning, the neocortex, can respond. This explains why, if you've ever been in a near death situation, you likely found yourself responding before you really understood the rationale behind your response. Your fight, flight, or freeze response took over so that *it* could be driving your brain rather than the part of your brain that needs to intellectually process information.[5]

Consider the options if my neocortex had engaged in a series of questions to assess my options while confronted with the bus:

Option 1—leave the bag on the curb and run across the street to beat the bus.

Option 2—take your bag with you back to the curb.

Option 3…by this time, I'm dead.

The amygdala helps ensure our safety by providing us an immediate reaction that shows up as fear, discomfort, or pain. This is how we know that there is a threat. These emotions are our early warning signs shouting, "Warning! Warning! You are entering dangerous territory!" Now, the problem is that not everything the amygdala perceives as a threat is real. At the airport walkway, the amygdala saved me from being hit by a bus, but in the conference room during a meeting (even though it feels like we are getting run over), the threat in the room is likely a differing opinion, not a bus. For many of us, our body will respond to the fear, discomfort, or pain in the meeting room as if it were warning us of a real physical threat. And we'll move to fight, flee, or freeze, regardless.[6]

We Think (We Process It Intellectually)

Once we feel pain, we move to engaging our neocortex, which then has time to think about what just happened. This part of the process is completely objective. Our brains are processing information about what occurred. In my scenario, once safe, I could acknowledge that I stepped out in front of a bus and stepped back with my bag before it could hit me. I then acknowledged that I was tired and not paying attention to where I was going as the probable cause of why I ended up in the situation. Back in the meeting room where we feel run over by a bus—our colleague who represents a threat—we can now intellectualize what has just occurred. This is when we collect data based on what we can see or hear.[7] Likely we might collect data that looks something like this:

- I asked for support from Robby before the meeting, and he agreed to go into this meeting aligned.
- Robby shared concerns to others in the room about my ideas.
- Others in the room agreed with Robby's concerns.

In and of itself, this data we observe and collect during this phase is benign.

We Feel Again (We Choose an Emotion)

Once we have had the opportunity to really scrutinize the situation with our intellect, we choose an emotion we want to hold on to. For example, after stepping out in front of the bus, I initially felt scared. I then analyzed the data and realized I had a contributing role by being sleepy and not paying attention. I then began to feel something else besides fear. I felt embarrassed. I mean, really, what was I thinking walking out in front of that bus without looking? Or maybe I could have chosen another emotion. I could have chosen anger projected onto others. How dare that bus driver! What was *he* thinking?

When we are faced with unpleasant emotions, we usually take one of two paths. We *blame in*, or we *blame out*. When we blame in, we turn our emotion inward and feel something about ourselves, taking on the weight of the information we have processed. These emotions include guilt, anger, disappointment, shame, helplessness, irritation, frustration, confusion, anxiety, worry, fear, concern, and more.

When we blame out, we turn our emotions outward and feel something toward others. The same range of emotions are available to us when we project them onto others as when we project them into ourselves. It's also important to know that this emotional choice is not mutually exclusive. We can feel something toward ourselves, as well as toward others, and we likely do. When we feel, think, then feel again, there is usually a lot going on at once and it is difficult to sort out. Some individuals don't even try to sort through the emotions firing in all directions. They just move to the next step, which is to react.

Before we study our reactions to our emotions, we need to further study the origin of our emotions. How exactly do we go from thinking with our neocortex to choosing an emotion? The process happens quickly, maybe not as quickly as the amygdala perceives a threat, but usually within minutes, we form a hypothesis and choose an emotion to go with it. We take that which is otherwise completely and totally objective, and we add meaning to further understand the situation.

Let's go back to the example of Robby in the meeting room. We know our immediate emotion is not a choice; the amygdala perceives a threat in milliseconds before our thinking mind, the neocortex, can engage. So we immediately feel pain, and the amygdala perceives Robby as the threat. Then, we process the situation with our thinking mind and evaluate what we can observe—the data, which in and of itself is completely objective. Then we feel again, but this time the emotion is projected toward Robby. As human beings, we are meaning-making machines. We do not leave the situation as data. Instead, we add meaning, which creates an emotion. The emotion we choose is based on the meaning we give the situation. Or said differently, the meaning we give to a situation creates the emotion we feel.

Let's say the meaning we give Robby's actions is that he is out for himself and looking to serve his own agenda. If that were the case, we would likely feel anger and bitterness toward him. But what if, instead, the meaning we give Robby's actions is that he forgot about what we talked about before the meeting and doesn't have all the necessary information he needs? If that were the meaning, we'd likely feel more curiosity than anger.

The question, then, when confronted by a primal emotional response followed by objective data, is "What do we make this mean to us?" This is our first opportunity to choose carefully, respectfully, and appropriately.

We Respond (We Choose Reaction or We Choose Action)

Depending on the emotions we choose, we set ourselves up for either action or reaction. If we choose an emotion that is constructive, such as curiosity, then we will likely soothe our fear and choose an action that moves us forward productively. If, on the other hand, we choose a destructive second layer of emotion, then we exacerbate our fear and move to reaction.

It is important to understand that reaction is not the same as courage. Reaction is an unhealthy coping strategy an individual uses to deal with tough times. Because the amygdala is the site of emotional learning, we learn to perceive whether something is a threat early on in our life. As a result, reaction becomes our most natural way to deal with tough times we have little or no control over.[8] To remedy this, we develop strategies to deal with the threats we face. If our strategy gets results, we keep using it. Unhealthy coping strategies take many forms and range from avoidance to aggression and everything in between. The problem is that, in leadership, reaction is not very effective—mostly because what we perceive to be a threat isn't always such. Although it may feel as if we are being run over by a bus in the middle of the team meeting, we are, in fact, not in any physical danger. Our physical safety is not at risk, only our fragile ego.

The first reactive leader I ever worked for was a middle-aged man with a meek stature but a forceful and belittling style. Let's call him Gerald. During the hiring process, I was continuously surprised that I kept getting called back for the next step. When we met, Gerald did not seem to like me much. He was gruff and disconnected during the interview and seemed frustrated by my answers. I left each of my three interviews with him feeling as if I had royally blown it. And yet, I was offered the job. I decided to take the position because of the opportunity for growth, a decision to this day I wonder about.

As it turned out, Gerald didn't just not like *me*; he didn't like people in general—or at least people whose views were different from his own. Gerald had one employee, however, whom he was very close to. The two of them would routinely discuss—in public—the performance of others on the team in a derogatory and unproductive manner. Many of the leadership team meetings consisted of the two of them sharing gossip about the happenings in the company. Those of us on the team were awkwardly placed in a position of either joining the gossip ring or staying out of it, which resulted in making us fodder for future gossip. It was a lot like being in the eighth grade actually, only we were all adults being paid to accomplish goals instead of working through the life lessons of an adolescent.

Although I'll never know for sure, it occurred to me years after working with Gerald that his belittling and gossiping nature seemed to stem more from insecurity than from a real disgust of others or even narcissism. He was caught up in gossip as a method of maintaining a position of importance over others. If he criticized and put down others, then the attention was on our faults rather than on his. I wish I had been able to see this then, but I was far too immature and took it personally. When Gerald was confronted with discomfort or pain, his reaction was to belittle others and gossip to deflect criticism. In doing so, he created discomfort and pain for others.

There are some organizational cultures that still exist today—too many, unfortunately—where aggressive, belittling, controlling, and manipulating coping strategies are used and get results. Why? Because those on the other end of the reaction also feel the need to protect themselves. They choose compliance as a strategy to stay safe, thus creating a false sense of safety and a false sense of results. These kinds of results are not sustainable. Leading is not about creating coping strategies in others. As a matter of fact, if we see others moving to fight, flight, or freeze and we don't intervene, we are inviting them to create coping strategies that get the results we want. On the surface, this may seem useful and even productive, but ultimately we have created a culture of fear and reaction. Creativity, high levels of problem solving, intuition, and other forms of excellence are not accessible when we are reacting.[9]

Sadly, when leaders continue to work from this place of reaction, team members become anesthetized to the stimulus and eventually feel nothing more than apathy or indifference. Apathy can show up in the form of lost productivity and focus. The threat the leader represents no longer has merit, and the coping strategy is no longer necessary; instead, the leader has created a team of zombies, armed with deadweight and mindless contribution. Sound familiar? It isn't long before even the leader finds himself drowning in apathy as well and is ready to give up.

Uncommon Choices

We have many choices about how to feel about the situation that presents itself to us and many choices about how to respond. However, we cannot access these options when we choose emotions that reinforce our body's natural inclination to move to a fight, flight, or freeze response. Therefore, improving this phase of our development is not easy. It requires great emotional fortitude and practice. It requires letting go of our coping strategies. It's important, however, not to be too hard on ourselves as we are learning this. I shared my story about Gerald, but "Gerald" could have been you or me. We all demonstrate reaction from time to time, some of us more than others.

Our common reaction to tough times is what makes us human, but our uncommon choices are what make us courageous.

The question is "Can we move to action in a way that is informed by the fear of discomfort or pain but is not led by the fear of discomfort or pain?" This is how courageous leaders move to action. Let's look at an example of action versus reaction.

Father Bob is the pastor of a church and the head of a top-rated private school. His school lives by an honor code that, like many organization's values and mission statements, is displayed on the walls throughout its building and in every classroom. The students recite it each morning after they say the Pledge of Allegiance.

"We will not lie, cheat, or steal."

"We will respect property, ours and that of others."

"We will respect the dignity of every human being."

Proudly, Father Bob can say that among his school's many accomplishments, his school received the sportsmanship award from the state athletic association for six straight years. In the middle of another thriving football season, it was brought to Father Bob's attention that two players on his team had yelled anti-Semitic remarks to another team's players. During an investigation, the accusations were corroborated by third-party witnesses. Not only did the two boys violate the honor code through their behavior, but other teammates also stood by and said nothing. Adding insult to injury, it was discovered that the entire team agreed to lie about the situation to protect the two players.

In Father Bob's eyes, the fact that the other boys did not discourage the behavior and then agreed to lie about it made every player guilty. As a result, he alerted the school's board that he wanted to cancel the rest of the football season. Parents made up most of the board, including some who had students who played on the football team. Reactions to his message shocked Father Bob, with some board members arguing that canceling the rest of the season would be counterproductive and cause more problems than it was worth. They shared data supporting the financial implications it would have if high-donor families were to remove their children from the school because of the decision. Additionally, some other parents who heard about the situation and Father Bob's proposal stormed into his office, ranting about the other team's improprieties and the injustice of the situation.

Take a moment and consider: If you were Father Bob, what would you do?

Father Bob decided to stick with his choice to cancel the football season even with the backlash and potential consequences the board warned him about. Two years later, the school is growing in donations and in enrollment. Although there were some parents who were not happy with the decision, there were many more parents who were grateful for Father Bob's strong leadership.

Using what we know now about feel-think-feel-act, let's look at the differences between Gerald's and Father Bob's choices and outcomes (see Table 1.1).

Table 1.1 Reaction Versus Action

Gerald's Reaction	Father Bob's Action
Feel: Discomfort and pain	Feel: Discomfort and pain
Think: I'm not good enough. Others will take advantage of my imperfections.	Think: Some parents and board members are sharing concerns about canceling the football season.
Feel: Insecurity and vulnerability	Feel: Curiosity, empathy for parents, concern for students' education
React: Belittle and gossip about others.	Action: Cancel the season.
Outcome: Discomfort and pain for others	Outcome: Strong message about the importance of values and overwhelming support from most parents and educators

A Message from Father Bob

We hang up signs, and we talk every day in our classrooms and in our chapel about respecting the dignity of every human being, yet it was this decision that was instrumental in teaching our students what this commitment really means. I don't regret it because the decision spoke a thousand words. It was the right thing to do.

When one considers a decision like this, you often have this inner voice that can paralyze you. You don't want to be disliked, you don't want to be confrontational, and you don't want to cause a disruption in your relationships with those you know and love. So instead you tell yourself that six months from now no one will care, so you don't do anything. You just let it go.

And that is the big temptation.

—Father Bob, pastor and head of school

The Big Temptation

When we give in to the temptation just to let an issue go rather than address it, we can expect one of two outcomes with regard to pain (see Figure 1.2).

In the avoid-create-avoid cycle, we avoid a situation to the point that we find ourselves feeling backed into a corner, and we eventually explode. When we do explode, we usually say and do things we later regret, so we tend to move back into avoidance, not wanting to re-create the same pain for ourselves and others. We avoid pain, create more pain, and then avoid pain again.

In the avoid-suppress-avoid cycle, we avoid a situation by never really addressing it, but instead hold in our opinions and words, and let the pain eat us up internally. Our frustration grows, and the problem remains unresolved. We avoid pain, suppress our pain, and avoid pain again.

Neither of these two outcomes produces sustainable, healthy results. Even though we alleviate our pain in the short term by not moving to action in the face of tough times, we create more pain for ourselves long term. If Father Bob had allowed the issues of disrespect and racial slurs to go unaddressed at his school, it would have saved him many headaches in the short term, but long term, it would have affected his credibility, the school's value system, and the students' education. Leaders have a responsibility to consider the impact of their action or inaction as it relates not only to them but also to the

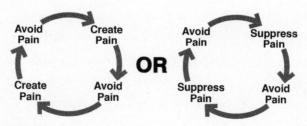

Figure 1.2 Pain Cycles

larger collective they lead. Let's look at another example of the Big Temptation in the workplace.

Marcus was a new manager who inherited a team of hourly workers who were padding their time sheets with hours not actually worked. When he realized that this was going on, he addressed the issue with each of his seven team members individually. Each one of them explained that this had become a common practice originated by his predecessor as a way to address the issue that they were underpaid. They all shared similar perspectives, explaining that because pay increases were difficult, if not impossible, to come by, this had become the most acceptable and easiest path to paying them what they were worth. Some told Marcus that this arrangement had been part of their informal interview and offer process, setting the expectation that they would be paid more than the hours they were actually working. When Marcus explained that padding time sheets was a violation of the company policy and had potentially serious consequences, not one of them expressed remorse for his or her actions but instead felt justified. To make matters more complicated, Marcus's predecessor was also his new boss. He now had ethical questions about the choices both his boss and his team members had made.

Marcus knew he could ignore the problem and let it continue. But he also knew that wasn't the kind of leader he wanted to be. A big problem faced him. He knew that addressing the problem would mean facing his boss, and he also wasn't sure how far up the chain the unethical behavior went. If he addressed the issue, it was possible that he would be opening himself up to retaliation on a larger scale. On the pain scale, he was at a 7—feeling overwhelmed—and could feel himself slipping into the Big Temptation just to let it go.

So, what is the solution for Marcus and others when faced with the Big Temptation? *Feel the pain, but do the right thing anyway.* Easier said than done, right? Not necessarily. Like Father Bob, Marcus was surprised to learn that when he addressed the issue rather than falling into the Big Temptation, good things followed. Not surprisingly, his boss was defensive at first, but Marcus continued to emphasize his goal of doing the right thing for the organization and the people rather than focusing on his boss's poor choices. A couple of days later, Marcus's boss agreed to meet with their senior leadership together to address the issue of fraudulent time sheets and rectify the situation as best as possible. In this scenario, Marcus's boss was given the opportunity to clean up the situation and address compensation through the proper procedures without any formal consequences. It was a humbling experience for him to be sure. He later told Marcus that he had learned much from Marcus during this situation and apologized for putting Marcus in a tough spot.

I realize not every story of doing the right thing has a happy ending. There are times when doing the right thing means suffering a tough consequence. *No good deed goes unpunished*, as the saying goes. But in the twilight of the day, after the laptops have been shut down and the employees have gone home, a question defines *The Courageous Leader*:

"Did I honor the courageous leader in me today, or did I give in to the Big Temptation?"

Honoring the Courageous Leader in You

To honor ourselves means we are willing to fulfill a commitment we have made to ourselves. To honor the courageous leader in you, you must first make a commitment to yourself to be willing to do the tough stuff in the face of discomfort and pain. Before you read any further, think about this and really consider this commitment. To what degree are you willing to do the tough stuff in the face of discomfort and pain (see Figure 1.3)?

I'm out sounds something like this…

"Not in this lifetime, lady. Take your courage and shove it where the sun don't shine."

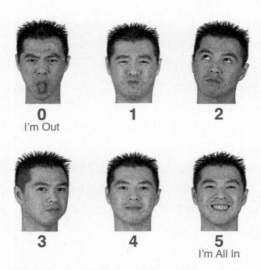

0
I'm Out

1

2

3

4

5
I'm All In

Figure 1.3 Commitment to Courage

I'm all in sounds something like this...

"I'm ready. I know I'm ready because I've considered the pain of not being courageous and it is significantly more than the pain or discomfort I might sustain by leading with a spine. I am willing to do the tough stuff even though it won't always be easy. I am committed to honoring the courageous leader in me for the benefit of others, the organization I lead, and myself."

You may not be ready to be all in. You might be somewhere between *I'm out* and *I'm all in*. That sounds something more like...

"I get that courage is important and I'm committed so long as I can really do it well."

This is a conditional response to courage—"I'm committed unless..." or "I'm committed until..." or "I'm going to try to give it my best shot..."

I'm going to sound a little bit like Yoda here, but there is no try, only do or do not when it comes to courage.[10] Courage is a mind-set that requires grit and determination. Doubt is the enemy of courage. Where doubt seeps in, courage erodes.

Having said that, it does not mean that by choosing *all in*, you have to do as Marcus did and confront your boss next week about an unethical choice. That kind of courage might just give you a heart attack or paralyze you indefinitely. That's not the goal here. It could be that, for you, being all in means being willing to take the first step, like sharing your ideas in a meeting when no one has asked for them but you know they would add value. That may be where you are ready to engage courage. Remember, pain is subjective, and it's up to the individual to determine what behaviors reach a tolerable pain threshold.

Assessing the Risks

Now I realize I just spent the last few paragraphs asking you to commit to courage, but before you do, it is important to assess the pros and cons of this choice. There are risks associated with courage, and knowing them is paramount to making an educated decision about your commitment to courage.

The risk of being courageous: We are vulnerable, we feel pain, and we are exposed.

The risk of *not* being courageous: We stop short of achieving our goals to the fullest.

At one point in my career, I was working for a construction materials company leading its talent development function, and I was tasked with creating an internal leadership development program. I was excited but also very scared. I had done the same thing in my previous organization but on a much smaller scale, and I had a team to support me and great people to learn from. At the construction company, I was initially a team of one, carrying a tremendous weight on my shoulders. If I succeeded, it would be a worthy accomplishment, but if I failed, the only person to blame would be me. I felt totally and completely exposed. On a pain scale, I was at about a 6. I was losing sleep and eating too much. I was definitely stressed out. I had a ton of unproductive questions swirling around, such as: "What if, in this process, people find out I'm not really all that talented? What if they think I'm a fraud? Am I a fraud?"

During the design process leading up to the execution of the leadership program, our company was acquired by a company based in Switzerland. As soon as the purchase was announced, I raced to the Internet to look up the company and learn as much as I could about its leadership and how it developed its people. The company was, in a word, impressive. I had a few speculative conversations with other team leaders, and we all agreed it was likely we would be rolled into the acquiring department's team. I had a moment of complete and total relief when I realized that if I did nothing, if I just gave up trying to launch a program internally, then I could just join this other team and help them—blend in, if you will—and could step out of the spotlight. I could let the people in this acquiring company take the lead. I could drag my feet for a few months until the dust settled, and that would be enough time to delay the project altogether. What a relief!

But as soon as the relief finished washing over me, I was left feeling disappointment and regret. I thought to myself, *If I don't do this now, it's possible I'll lose the opportunity altogether and risk not being able to create and contribute something significant.* In a matter of minutes, I went from relief to disappointment to resolve. I chose to honor the courageous leader in me and get moving. If the acquiring company was going to pull the plug on the project, there was nothing I could do to stop it, but I wasn't going to hide from this opportunity. I was going to give it all I had and hope that I could make a difference with my work.

As it turns out, I was able to launch that program and many more to come after that. Several years later, I honored the courageous leader in me again by launching a leadership development company with my business partner, and we created Personify Leadership, a program that is now being distributed globally.

In business, if achieving more with less is the goal—as it certainly seems to be—achieving your fullest potential is your greatest tool to thrive. There is no other way to reach our fullest potential or achieve our most profound goals in life than to put ourselves out there and embrace the pain. The risk in being courageous is real, but so are the results that follow.

Chapter Application

Questions to Consider

1. What is your pain threshold when faced with tough situations or people?
2. What situations or people are most uncomfortable for you?
3. Do you find that, when faced with tough situations or people, you tend to react, or are you careful to think things through and instead move to action?
4. When faced with the Big Temptation, do you tend to avoid, create, and avoid pain or avoid, suppress, and avoid pain?
5. Is your strategy for dealing with the Big Temptation getting you the results you would like? If not, how might you change your approach to be more successful?

Strategies to Practice

1. Take a moment to plan how you want to act (instead of react) the next time you're faced with a challenging person or situation that seems to be troubling you.

2. Breathing is a powerful tool to keep us thinking instead of reacting. It brings oxygen in and pushes against the chemicals pulsing through our bodies. When you're faced with tough times, practice breathing more consciously.

3. Practicing being courageous during tough times actually increases our tolerance for pain and builds our courage muscle. The more we move to action (not reaction) and experience success, the less discomfort or pain we feel being courageous. Practice is the key!

Notes

1.   "Anais Nin Quotes." Excerpt from THE DIARY OF ANAIS NIN, Volume Three: 1939-1944. Copyright © 1969 by Anais Nin and renewed 1997 by Rupert Pole and Gunther Stuhlmann. Reprinted by permission of Houghton Mifflin Harcourt Publishing Company.

2.   Ross, Philip. "Why Do Some People Tolerate Pain Better Than Others? New Study Links Pain Sensitivity with Grey Matter in Brain." *International Business Times*, January 15, 2014. http://www.ibtimes.com/why-do-some-people-tolerate-pain-better-others-new-study-links-pain-sensitivity-grey-matter-brain.

3.   Wake Forest University Baptist Medical Center. "Brain Imaging Confirms That People Feel Pain Differently." *ScienceDaily*, June 24, 2003. www.science-daily.com/releases/2003/06/030624090043.htm.

4.   Institute for Health and Human Performance. "Performing Under Pressure: The Science of Emotional Intelligence" (training program). Accessed December 22, 2016. http://www.ihhp.com/emotional-intelligence-training/.

5.   Öhman, Arne. "The Role of the Amygdala in Human Fear: Automatic Detection of Threat." *Psychoneuroendocrinology* 30, no. 10 (November 2005): 953–58.

6.   Koutsikou, Stella, Jonathan J. Crook, Emma V. Earl, J. Lianne Leith, Thomas C. Watson, Bridget M. Lumb, and Richard Apps. "Neural Substrates Underlying Fear-Evoked Freezing: The Periaqueductal Grey–Cerebellar Link." *The Journal of Physiology* 592, Part 10 (May 2014): 2197–213.

7. Wright, Anthony. "Limbic System: Amygdala." In *Neuroscience Online: An Electronic Textbook for the Neurosciences,* edited by John H. Byrne. Houston: University of Texas Medical School at Houston, 1997. http://neuroscience .uth.tmc.edu/s4/chapter06.html.

8. Clark, Gregory A. "Emotional Learning: Fear and Loathing in the Amygdala." *Current Biology* 5, no. 3 (March 1995): 246–8.

9. Amabile, Teresa, Constance N. Hadley, and Steven J. Kramer. "Creativity Under the Gun." *Harvard Business Review* 80, no. 8 (August 2002): 52–61.

10. Lucas, George, Mark Hamill, Harrison Ford, and Carrie Fisher. *Star Wars: Episode V – The Empire Strikes Back*, DVD. Directed by Irvin Kershner. Los Angeles: 20th Century Fox, 1980.

2 The Courage to Get Unstuck

In the middle of the road of my life I awoke in a dark wood where the true way was wholly lost.[1]

—Dante

You know that feeling when everything is going exactly as you want it? You awake excited and passionate about your day. The sun is shining and the birds are singing. On your way to work you hit all the green lights while your favorite song plays on the radio. At lunch, your boss's boss asks you to join her at your favorite restaurant because she wants to get to know you better and understand your career goals. Your afternoon is full of productive conversations with exactly whom you want to talk to at exactly the right time. Your day flows like that all the way back home, where you have a package from a loved one waiting at your doorstep and your spouse greeting you with an open bottle of your favorite wine. You sink into your bed staring into the night sky, grateful for the tranquility you feel before you close your eyes. There is nothing more you could ask for. Life is seamless. Life is good.

Now that you have that feeling of being in the flow of life, imagine the exact opposite. Imagine you are moving as fast as you can with all your energy and might in a large pool of quicksand, and you're going nowhere. You are stuck. Living out the same old pattern over and over with little to no success, feeling incremental to no movement forward, just waiting for the next thing to reveal itself. Lethargic, exhausted, and lonely.

I know the feeling of "stuckness" very well. When I was 24 and a first-time entrepreneur, I started an online recruiting company for the hotel industry with several leaders of a hospitality marketing company. Building our company was thrilling. The first year was one home run after another. We had cash, little debt, and almost immediate industry credibility. In my personal life, I was young and adventurous, yet I had lived, worked, and gone to college all within the same 45-mile radius. I felt like I knew everyone and found the familiarity exhilarating. Then, something changed. The success of our business began to dry up. Instead of consistent big wins, we started suffering one loss after another until we were on life support and began our first round of capital calls. In my personal life, the once stimulating familiarity of my hometown began to feel confining. Everywhere I turned there was a guy I had dumped or who had dumped me. My friends were getting married and moving to the suburbs to start families, and the idea of doing the same felt like a prison sentence with no chance for parole.

I didn't understand what was happening to me. Luckily, I had a psychologist for a neighbor. She was 30 years my senior and liked to drink martinis on her back porch at sunset. One Friday afternoon I took over a bottle of McCormick vodka (it was all I could afford at the time) and asked whether she was up for a chat. I shared with her the quizzical shift occurring in my life and asked her to help me sort it out.

"Seems clear to me," she said, tipping back her martini glass and gulping the cheap vodka. "Your life is kicking you out of it. It's time to move on."

My life was kicking me out? Whatever did that mean? There was no amount of vodka that could help me figure that out. I had so much invested in the life choices I had made thus far. What did she mean "move on"? I brushed it off until several weeks later, when her words came back to me while I was reading a seemingly unrelated book.

I was standing in the middle of a Barnes & Noble, having plucked a book by Charlene Belitz and Meg Lundstrom from the shelf, and was skimming through it with no real intention. I landed on a page that talked about a woman who had felt stuck in her life for many years, in both a bad marriage and limited career. She sold everything she had and moved to Denver. She described the beauty of the city and the way life unfolded for her when she arrived there. As I was reading through the pages, swaying in place, I accidently bumped into a man with beads in his long hair who wore old sandals.

"I love that book, man," he said, leaning over me. "I read it on the plane ride back from Colorado."

"You just got back from Colorado?" I asked, completely unsure why I cared other than the serendipity of the situation.

"Yeah, skied for seven days. It was awesome!" he said.

"I thought about moving there once. I have a good friend from college who went there, but I don't know anyone else. I don't even know how to ski," I said. Why was I telling him this?

"Who cares, you'll learn. You should move, man," he said and then added, "Definitely buy the book."

"Thank you," I said and moved over to the next aisle to think about the eerie coincidence of reading a story about a woman who was stuck like me and changed her life by moving to Denver while bumping into a man who had not only read the book but also had done so on his way back from Colorado. Then there was the title of the book: *The Power of Flow: Practical Ways to Transform Your Life with Meaningful Coincidence.*[2] It was one of those times that make you stop and think.

Then, something even more outrageous happened. My phone rang, and while digging it out of my purse, I saw that the number was out of state and one I didn't recognize. I answered it anyway. On the other end was my college girlfriend who had just moved to Denver.

"Ang, it's me! I'm calling you right now from the Rocky Mountains. You have to move here. You would love it!" I dropped the phone.

I got the message. I understood that my life was kicking me out and something much better in Colorado was waiting for me. Six months later, I moved to Denver and took on a leadership role in human resources that allowed me to slow down and learn some of the tricks of the trade before trying to master a start-up company. I learned to ski, made new friends whose phase of life aligned with mine, and met my future husband. I was in the flow again.

When we stay too long in the wrong place, waiting, unwilling to budge, stuck in our old routines, life will make an effort to kick us out. We feel that first kick like a small twinge of pain, but after a while it grows and intensifies. This pain is often an indicator that it's time to make a shift, a signal that it's time to create change. The more we resist, the more stuck we become and the more pain we feel.

When Life Kicks You out of the Workplace

Lester was a company man, loyal to a fault. He started with his company as an intern and over a 20-year period led several corporate teams, moved to three new states, and took on growing responsibility with company acquisitions. He never complained. He loved his work and he loved his company. But after years of being the *acquiring* company, Lester's company was now being acquired itself and experiencing layoffs. He worried he would be let go during the first round of restructuring, but instead was promoted to take on even more responsibility. He found himself working what felt like long, endless hours. He would often wake in the middle of the night thinking about work and unable to get back to sleep. In spite of his effort and achievements, he was feeling stuck. When he started out as an intern

20 years prior, his goal was to be the company CEO. His vision for this was closer than ever, but something just didn't seem to fit anymore. He was happy, but he wasn't passionate. He didn't feel himself growing anymore. He wasn't sure he wanted to stay in a leadership role, and he wasn't even sure he wanted to stay in the industry. However, Lester wasn't one to shake things up. So he continued to plug along until the day his company did an exhaustive second round of layoffs that left Lester unemployed for the first time in his career. It was shocking, yet also a relief. Lester shared with me that he would likely never have made the change himself. He would have continued to work for his company and to ignore his feelings of frustration and growing discontentment. Now, he had options.

Several weeks after Lester was laid off, an old boss from a previous company found him and made him an offer to come to his company. It was an almost identical role at a competing company, working for a team he had already worked with and knew well. Lather. Rinse. Repeat. He knew it was the safe play because he had already done the job for many years. Instead of saying yes and falling back into the same pattern he was in before, Lester honored the courageous leader in him and turned the job down. He stayed in the job market for several more months, testing out other opportunities, and ended up partnering with an industry leader in a start-up entrepreneurial environment. For the first time in his career, he would be working for himself and growing a business.

When you stay stuck, sometimes life doesn't kick you out but leaves you behind.

Sandra was different from Lester. She wasn't looking to take on a leadership role or be the CEO; she liked her comfortable and steady role in quality control. Rather than climbing the corporate ladder, she preferred to stay under the radar and was unwilling to take on more responsibility. She was known for being exceptionally gifted in many areas of leadership, as well as her technical skills. Even though she was humble and avoided praise, she was flooded with it by her peers, her leadership, and her customers. Her boss had asked her many times to consider taking on a more formal leadership role, but she resisted. Deep down, Sandra knew she was not content and that she was not growing, but she feared that if she took on more responsibility, she would fail, and she didn't want to let others down. It was easier if she just stayed in place.

Eventually her boss and others stopped asking her to step up, and she was left to do what she felt comfortable doing. No more, no less. Over the next couple of years, the company grew, but Sandra did not. Many around her were promoted to roles of increasing responsibility. Sandra found herself now working for others who were less competent and capable than she, and slowly she felt herself becoming resentful and restless. In addition, she was underperforming and she knew it. She just wasn't motivated to bring her best self to work each day. It finally hit her hard one day when she had lunch with a colleague who had just recently been promoted to a senior leadership role. Sandra had started as a peer to this colleague 10 years previously, but now he was accelerating. She realized life had left her behind. Seeing herself in contrast with her colleague helped Sandra realize that her choice to stay on the safe path had created more pain than she would have felt if she had moved out of her comfort zone. Sandra told me it was then she decided to do the work necessary to take on more responsibility. Six years later, I met up with Sandra, who was flourishing in a regional leadership role. Her former peer had been promoted again, leaving a spot for her to be promoted into his role, as CEO for her company's global supply division.

Moving on or Going Deeper

Getting unstuck is good, and change is good. But what happens when the options for change are different? By moving to Colorado, I learned the importance of moving on when life kicks you out. But now, 16 years later, I've felt my life kicking me out again, but in different ways. I just turned 40 and have a loving husband, two amazing children, one thriving business, and one growing business. Everything is good but not good enough. It's taken me a while to sort through my feelings of being stuck. This time, the pain of being stuck was easier to identify but harder to solve. I love my family, I love my community, and I love my work, yet my current circumstances are not fulfilling me the way they used to. Something has to change. Getting up and moving to another state to start all over again just didn't make sense the way it did when I was 25. I had to find another solution. What I have learned, after months of inward reflection, is that some kinds of stuck don't require moving on, but instead, going deeper.

Going deeper is about finding ways to take the current life experiences you have to the next level, at work, at home, and in your community. Going deeper in its most simplistic terms is about becoming curious all over again about the things that are already in your life and exploring them with a renewed passion. At work, that could mean taking on new and expansive responsibilities or broadening your network of contacts in the industry or moving to a new product line. It could mean taking an advanced certification that enriches your expertise in your field. It could mean seeking out a mentor. The list of ways to go deeper is endless when you finally commit to making a change to your current situation.

I work with a lot of leaders who have been at their companies for many years and are wondering whether they should move on or go deeper. The answer to this question is not an easy one. It's very personal. When your life kicks you out, it doesn't always specify how to change, only that you must change. Because this is a personal question, I can answer this only with the wisdom that's come from my own personal experiences.

Lesson 1: Ask the right question. Rather than asking the question "Should I stay in this role (this company, this relationship, this community), or should I move on?" ask yourself, "What will bring me the greatest growth that is in my control to change?"

Lesson 2: Trust the process. As tempted as you might be, don't rush the process of determining whether to move on or go deeper. If you don't have the answer, then you don't have the answer. You can't force the elusive butterfly to land on you until it's ready.

Lesson 3: Seek clarity, not absolute certainty. When you start down this path, seek clarity for yourself and what you want, but don't make absolute certainty your goal. None of us likes ambiguity about important things in our lives, but expecting absolute certainty can send you spiraling into the abyss of ambiguity, rather than saving you from it. Clarity, on the other hand, is available to us in time and with reflective experience. In some cases, when life kicks you out, the answers are as obvious as they were for me when I moved to Colorado. And in other cases, the answers are subtler, as they have been for me this past year. Regardless of how the answers come, they do come. You just have to acknowledge the pain, be open to change, and ask the right questions.

Going Deeper in Action

Not too long after I wrote the story I shared here about my personal experience of getting stuck, moving to Colorado, and later choosing to go deeper, I posted the story to my blog. One of my good friends and thought partners, Sergio, e-mailed me and shared his appreciation for the story. He, too, had been struggling with being stuck. Sergio was a director at a national building products company. He really loved his position early on. The way he described it, he had a seat at the table with the leadership team. He felt valued and was able to do compelling and interesting work. That changed, however, when leadership changed and he found himself in an environment in which it was unclear how the organization wanted to leverage him and his team. After reading my blog, he e-mailed me and shared how the idea of going deeper was really powerful for him. He said it gave him another way of viewing his situation and a way to embrace his circumstances. I was very excited to hear that there was such an immediate application for Sergio that made his work life experience more desirable.

Several months later, Personify Leadership decided to create a new position. We felt Sergio would be an excellent fit for it. He was a stellar person and top-notch professional. Any company would be privileged to have him join its team. I couldn't wait to call him and offer him the job. I took him to lunch to get a sense of his interest level before begging him to come work with us. Sergio was humbled by our interest and, regrettably, turned us down. He explained that, although he had been looking for opportunities outside of his company, ironically, after applying the message of going deeper, he felt that staying put and exploring his current position further was now the best way to go. He had begun to feel a change in how he was approaching his work that made him excited to see what else might develop with his current company. I did try to coax him to make another decision, of course, but he stuck to his guns. I realized then, honoring the courageous leader in him that had chosen to go deeper was far more important than having him join our team.

Stuck in a Paradigm

Pari and I began working together on a coaching basis because she was seeking assistance in defining her next goal. She was having difficulty getting clear about where she should take her career, and she was feeling rather stifled. Similar to me, Pari was very happy with her family, her community, and her work but was feeling the jabbing pains of being stuck. After interviewing Pari's teammates and leadership, it was clear that she was viewed as a strong leader with incredible potential to do just about anything she wanted. The problem was that Pari wasn't sure what that was.

To help Pari gain more clarity, I had her create a "life line." I asked Pari to recall all the important times in her life, from the time she was born to the present. I told her to consider the people and situations that were significant to her and to explain how they shaped her life today.

Pari's story starts in a small town in India. Her father had been stationed there for work. It was a town too small to provide a good education, so she went to live with her grandparents at the age of five. Although you might presume this was a sad time in Pari's life, it was quite the opposite. She says she felt nothing but love from her grandparents and the extended family who lived nearby. She grew up very happy and content. It wasn't until her beautiful cousin joined their family in town that things changed. As she recounts, her cousin wasn't just beautiful; she was exceptional. Her blue eyes and fair skin were not only rare but also adored. Pari's brown eyes would never be blue, and her dark skin would never be light. For the first time in her life, she felt stuck. She felt motivated to do something exceptional. So she went on a mission to find whatever *exceptional* was for her.

Pari joined a dance team and learned to dance. She auditioned for a part in a big show but got the understudy position. She stuck with it, and when a spot on the team opened up, she was selected to perform. That's when she realized she could dance. Really dance. She was exceptional. She remembers that, during the performance, her cousin left the room with a look of envy on her face. Pari was pleased. Now, it wasn't just Pari who was jealous of her cousin, but her cousin was jealous of her, too. She felt validated.

Many years later, Pari's cousin went on to win a beauty pageant hosted by the town. It just so happened that Pari's college was also hosting a beauty pageant, so she entered. Although she had no real desire to perform in a beauty pageant, she was once again motivated by the desire not to be less than someone else, especially her cousin. The pageant had three parts. The first was an introduction, the second a catwalk, and the third a question presented by the judge. She knew she would not perform well on the catwalk. She just wasn't the kind to dress provocatively and saunter down a runway. The question, of course, was random and not something she could prepare for in advance. She figured her only real shot at winning was to have a stunning introduction. Pari prepared and practiced, and on the night of the performance, instead of wearing the customary evening gown, she wore a traditional Indian dress to signify her independence and express her cultural heritage. As she had hoped, her introduction and the answer to their question blew the judges away, and she won. Once again she felt validated.

Since that time, Pari has moved to the United States and established a career as a high-performing professional at a Fortune 500 company, and she is married with children. Everything is great, except that it isn't because she just doesn't know what that next big thing is for her. That's partly because Pari's not just stuck in her life; she's also stuck in her paradigm.

In the past, Pari's primary source of motivation came from comparing herself to others and seeing where she came up short, then competing with all her might to prevail. Peter Senge, author of *The Fifth Discipline*, describes what Pari was feeling as "creative tension." When *where we want to be* is different from *where we are*, creative tension is the force that brings the two together.[3] For Pari, proving herself to others was the source of her creative tension. Now that she was at a place in life where she had all the right things and no one obvious to prove herself to, she didn't know where to go next. This is not an unusual place for leaders to find themselves. When the world around us changes and we don't change our paradigm, we often find ourselves stuck and lacking creative tension.

After sorting through this further, Pari concluded that she wanted to know more about what she was good at rather than seeking to compete and prevail. So she began using some of the tools for getting unstuck.

Instead of asking, "What is someone else doing that I'm not, and how can I compete to prove my worth?" she asked herself the question "What is it I can do to contribute in a meaningful way and give my best to others?" Her entire focus became about doing something that would add value for others, *not* doing something that would make her look better than someone else. She described her new vision for herself as wanting to start her day with a cup of coffee and a newspaper, feeling a great sense of satisfaction for having contributed her strengths in a positive way that helped others.

We started down the path of becoming clearer about what it is that she does so well that brings value to others. Pari began to see that the things she does naturally are considerable strengths, and instead of talking about whether she should move on from her role or her company, the conversation began to shift toward discovering how to leverage her strengths more consistently in the work she does today. When we wrapped up our work together, Pari found herself in a place where she was far more confident in herself, and she was exploring opportunities on the job and in her company to expand her contribution. She was able to get unstuck and go deeper.

Pain During the Transition

Although discomfort and pain are early warning signs that we are stuck, we often stay there, enduring the pain because we anticipate that the discomfort or pain of making the transition to something new will be even greater. So we stay in a bad place, telling ourselves that the alternative is worse, when in reality the alternative is what holds more pleasure and more possibility—we just have to make the transition from one to the other. Getting unstuck requires the courage to experience discomfort and pain during the transition. This phenomenon of human behavior hit me during a seemingly normal everyday occurrence with my then three-year-old.

During a winter business trip, on which I had brought my kids, Cate found warmth and comfort in the hotel bathtub. She heard the doorbell ring and the hotel attendant bring in room service. She told me she wanted to eat. I explained to her that dinner was ready but that she needed to hop out of the tub and get dressed. She began to sob uncontrollably and said, "Mom, that will never work. I'm too cold and the water is what is keeping me warm."

I reiterated that, as soon as she got out of the tub, I would dry her off and put her in warm clothes, and she would be warm and able to eat. She sobbed some more and said, "But Mom, I'm so hungry!" Once again, I pointed out how easy it would be to get out and get her food. She said, "Yeah, but if I get out of the tub, I'll be really, really cold."

Cate's current state was warm and hungry. Cate's desired state was warm and full. The only way she could get from her current state to her desired state was to temporarily be cold and hungry, a seemingly worse off scenario. And this is how we get and stay stuck. We sit in the comfort of our situation and hunger for something more.

Suspended between our current situation and the situation we desire, we experience the pain of the transition like a trapeze artist swinging from one bar to the next. William Bridges, a best-selling author and expert in the field of change management, refers to this transition as the move from the ending of one thing through the neutral zone to the beginning of something new. He describes change as fast and the transition through the neutral zone as something that takes time.

He defines transitions as the dynamic interludes between stages of development that function to close out one phase, reorient, and renew people for the next phase. He also defines four Laws of Organization Development that apply during these transitions from one phase to another. Bridges' Laws were designed to describe expected behavior of organizations during transition. Here are the four laws from Bridges's work (amended slightly) to reflect the more personal experience of change:

First Law of Organization Development. Those who were most at home with the necessary activities and arrangements of one phase are the ones who are the most likely to experience the subsequent phase as a severe personal setback.

Second Law of Organization Development. The successful outcome of any phase of personal development triggers personal demise by creating challenges that you are not yet equipped to handle.

Third Law of Organization Development. In any significant transition, the thing the individual needs to let go of is the very thing that has got him or her this far.

Fourth Law of Organization Development. Whenever there is a painful, troubled time for an individual, a developmental transition is probably going on.[4]

How incredibly powerful these laws are for describing the reality of getting unstuck. I don't know about you, but I feel as if William Bridges has followed me and half of the world's population around for decades and documented the realities of our lives in his research. His words are accurate and insightful, and more important, they present an opportunity.

If we can anticipate that these four laws will surface in our courageous development as they do in organization development, then when they do come up, instead of resisting them, we can view them as signposts, alerting us to alternative paths forward.

If we can anticipate pain and discomfort as part of the transitional process, then when it develops, we can embrace it rather than fight it and make it worse.

Making Sense of Our Pain

Sometimes we stay stuck because we can't find meaning or because of the meaning we provide our circumstances. If we are unaware of this, over time, our feelings of pain can translate to feelings of despair. Chip Conley, a former CEO and now best-selling author, wrote a book called *Emotional Equations*.[5] He identified an equation for describing what it feels like to be in our stuckness:

Despair = Suffering – Meaning

Conley attributes this equation to Viktor Frankl, a man who survived concentration camps, tested the theory that meaning can keep people alive, and went on to write *Man's Search for Meaning*. In an interview with Ken Page from *Psychology Today*, Conley describes how he uses Frankl's equation.

> Let me explain the "sacred algebra." If you're going through a period of suffering, like Victor Frankl in a concentration camp, or me in my own mental prison, it's as though everything is going wrong, as though you're in a downward spiral. When you're in that place in life, suffering does feel like a constant.
>
> If you believe in Buddhist philosophy and thinking, the first noble truth of Buddhism is that suffering is ever present. So think of suffering as the constant. Think of meaning as the variable. If you remember back to algebra, there is often a constant and a variable in an equation. If suffering remains the constant, then when you increase meaning (the variable) despair goes down.
>
> Despair equals suffering minus meaning.
>
> Let me do the simple math so that it makes sense.... $8 = 10 - 2$. Despair (8) equals suffering (10) minus meaning (2).
>
> $8 = 10 - 2$.
>
> So if meaning goes up from 2 to 3, the despair goes down from 8 to 7.
>
> When meaning goes up, despair goes down. This equation helped me to see that meaning and despair are somewhat inversely proportional, so the more I could find meaning in my life, the more I would reduce my despair.[6]

Using *The Courageous Leader* language, I'm going to change this equation slightly and substitute *suffering* with the word we've been using to describe suffering:

Despair = Pain – Meaning

If pain is the constant, then to live a life avoiding pain is futile. It is a natural part of the human condition. But to live with it, we have to make sense of it. If we can make sense of it, then we get unstuck, and we move into the flow of life. If we can make sense of it, we will grow and change the equation to be:

Pain + Meaning = Growth

One American hero and iconic leader brings this equation to life for us in how he lives his meaning. In 1967, John McCain was a U.S. Navy pilot flying over North Vietnam when his aircraft was shot down, and he was taken captive by the Vietnamese. He was held captive for five and a half years. He was badly beaten and was not provided much in the way of medical care in the early stages of his captivity. On several occasions, he was offered release from captivity, but he refused to leave if others were not also released with him. Although his circumstances improved over time, he continued to suffer beatings and inadequate care during that time. In an article published by the *U.S. News & World Report* in May of 1973, he described the meaning he gave his experience in his own words. He said, "I had a lot of time to think over there and came to the conclusion that one of the most important things in life—along with a man's family—is to make some contribution to his country."[7]

It was clear that McCain experienced a great amount of pain, yet at every opportunity to eliminate the pain and leave the camp, he refused. He viewed his pain as an opportunity to demonstrate his allegiance to his fellow prisoners and to his country.

McCain has gone on to lead a successful life outside those prison walls as an influential leader in Congress known for his integrity and patriotism, and as an advocate for ending waterboarding as an interrogation technique. The meaning he found during his time of pain transformed his experience into something he could learn from and share with others. If he had given in to despair, it's likely he would have come home sooner but not with the honor and integrity that he believed in. The meaning he attached to his experience transformed the way he approached his captivity and the life he chose to live as a prisoner and after.

Growth takes courage. If you want to stay stuck, then stay put and wait for someone else to do the heavy lifting. If you want transformational change in your life that brings about temporary pain *and* lasting growth, determine what has you stuck, determine what meaning you want to give it, and then make a choice to move on or go deeper.

Chapter Application

Questions to Consider

1. Where am I stuck?
2. What am I afraid to let go of?
3. What am I afraid of experiencing in the transition?
4. What can I do to reduce the pain of the transition from my current state to my desired state?
5. What is my vision of a successful new beginning?
6. What is the benefit of my new beginning?
7. What do I need to do to honor the courageous leader in me to make it to my new beginning?

Strategies for Getting Unstuck

1. If you're unsure about whether to move on or go deeper:
   a. Ask the right question.
   b. Trust the process.
   c. Seek clarity, not absolute certainty.
2. If you want to get unstuck, you'll need to accept that pain is part of the transition and that you will be cold and hungry as part of the process.
3. Pain + Meaning = Growth. During the transition from cold and hungry to warm and full, remember the meaning (or use this time to find your meaning) behind your decision to make a change.

Notes

1. Alighieri, Dante. *The Divine Comedy: The Inferno, the Purgatorio, and the Paradiso.* Translated by John Ciardi. New York: New American Library, 2003.

2. Belitz, Charlene, and Meg Lundstrom. *The Power of Flow: Practical Ways to Transform Your Life with Meaningful Coincidence.* New York: Three Rivers Press, 1998.

3. Senge, Peter M. *The Fifth Discipline: The Art & Practice of the Learning Organization.* New York: Doubleday, 1990.

4. *Managing Transitions: Making the Most of Change* by William Bridges, copyright © 1991. Reprinted with permission from Da Capo Press, an imprint of Perseus Books, LLC, a subsidiary of Hachette Book Group, Inc.

5. Conley, Chip. *Emotional Equations: Simple Truths for Creating Happiness + Success.* New York: Atria, 2012.

6. Page, Ken. "Chip Conley: Emotional Equations, Love and Meaning." *Finding Love* (blog), *Psychology Today.com*, October 7, 2012. https://www.psychologytoday.com/blog/finding-love/201210/chip-conley-emotional-equations-love-and-meaning.

7. McCain, John S. "John McCain, Prisoner of War: A First-Person Account." *U.S. News & World Report*, January 28, 2008. http://www.usnews.com/news/articles/2008/01/28/john-mccain-prisoner-of-war-a-first-person-account.

3 The Courage to Take a Stand

We do not act rightly because we have virtue or excellence, but we rather have those because we have acted rightly.[1]

—Aristotle

Daniel was having a really big year. His once small-town, laid-back business was growing dramatically thanks to one client in particular. The client, although difficult to deal with, was expanding its operations and needed Daniel's team to help it grow. For Daniel, this meant lots of additional revenue. Over $2 million annually, to be more specific. Everyone on Daniel's team was excited except for Oscar, who was responsible for dealing directly with the client daily. He didn't see this as a big win at all but rather more work and frustration for him. One day, when the growth surge was creating pressure for everyone, the client stormed into the office, marched straight to Oscar, pointed a finger at his face, and began berating him. When Oscar tried to leave the room, the client grabbed him by the arm and forced him into a chair, ordering, "You'll listen to what I have to say!" As the client verbally abused him in the middle of the office, Oscar's peers watched in silence.

Daniel was stunned and remained silent. Finally, the client finished his tirade and left the office, slamming the door behind him. Everyone on the team looked at Daniel, who didn't know what to say or do, so he slipped into his office and closed the door, leaving Oscar to lick his wounds alone.

On a pain scale of 1 to 10, I think it's safe to say Daniel was likely hovering toward the upper end. Like this situation with the client, any number of scenarios that cause us pain and challenge us to be courageous may present themselves in the normal course of a workday. As in this situation with Daniel, some of them require the courage to take a stand.

To take a stand is *to choose action in tough times that reflects our leadership values*. It isn't enough to say this is what I believe in; this is what is important to me. Courageous leaders align their values with their behaviors. Being aware of who you truly are and what you want to be to others is critical to knowing when taking a stand is necessary.

So, What Exactly Are Values?

Values are the driving motivation behind our behaviors. They are the *why* we choose to act in a certain way. Research shows that from early on in our development, we start learning right from wrong and begin making decisions about what is important to us. Our family, friends, culture, ethnicity, and other environmental factors influence and assist us in shaping who we have become.[2–4] Let's look at some examples of how values develop.

Missy, a branch manager for an agricultural inspection company, possesses incredibly high standards and a very strong work ethic. For Missy, these values came from growing up in a family where her father and mother both worked—and worked hard. At an early age, she went to work for her father, dutifully assisting him in his home-based business. She watched him work endless hours to accommodate the needs of his customers. Often, she'd come home from school to find customers lined up outside the door, waiting for him to help them. Her father wasn't the only one in town with this business, but he was the one people preferred to come to. He was a perfectionist who would work long hours, often seven days a week, to meet the demands of his business. It's no surprise, then, that one of Missy's overriding leadership values is a strong work ethic.

Kim is senior vice president of a nonprofit organization. Although she values hard work, her most prominent values are peace and well-being. When she was young, her parents did not get along. But not in the way that most of us imagine when we think about fighting parents. Her parents avoided each other, actually living in separate parts of their home. Kim describes coming home from school each day facing the painstaking decision of which parent to see first. If she chose her mom, then she would upset her dad. If she chose her dad, then she upset her mom. Every day felt like a losing battle. She translates that today into being a leader who values peace and well-being for others. However, she has to be careful not to try to solve others' problems for them but rather allow them to find their own solutions and their own paths to peace and well-being.

I can personally relate to these stories. There are very important people in my life who helped shape my values as well. Throughout high school and most of college, I worked for a man named Bob (who, ironically, owned a restaurant named Paul's Burgers and Shakes). Bob was a quiet, reserved older man, and what I remember about him most was his incredibly gracious and charitable nature. On more than one occasion, Bob wrote checks to employees to help supplement their education or assist them in buying a car. I always thought his charity came because of his loyalty to us as his employees. I realized after an unexpected event that his charity extended far beyond loyalty.

One summer, Bob hired two relatively unknown, local boys who had dropped out of school when they were 14 and had jumped from job to job to make ends meet. None of the other employees really knew these two, and we thought they were suspicious characters, to say the least. Nonetheless, Bob hired them. During the first few months, they came in when they were scheduled, worked hard, and generally kept to themselves. Then one morning when I came in early to assist in opening the restaurant, I found Bob sitting inside, looking disappointed. When I asked him what was wrong, he said that someone had stolen money from the restaurant overnight. He continued, stating that he believed it was the two boys because they had a key to the building, had access to the safe, and had not shown up to work that day. Boiling with anger, I shouted, "Call the police now. They need to see this and get them!" He responded calmly, "Angela, if they took that money from me, they needed it more than I do." I was astounded. How could they do such a thing? But for Bob, charity was his value, and that value was worth far more to him than $1,000 taken from the safe.

Bob's courage to take a stand for what he believed in inspired the value of charity in me. I give without thinking now in every aspect of my life, whether it be in business, at home, in my community, or in my travels. Whenever I have the chance to give, out comes my wallet, my heart, and my support.

Actual and Aspirational Values

We've determined that our values come from early life lessons and the core of who we are, but that does not mean that our values are not also evolving. We are not molds cast and left to dry. We are a living, breathing work of art that is continuously being sculpted and refined.

For example, if you were to ask me what was important to me before I had children, I would have had a very different answer from what I would say today. It's not that the person I was then is not who I am today; it's just that the person I was then was not complete. Adding a family to my life brought responsibility and complexity that changed the lens through which I view the world. My values from 10 years ago have evolved because I have evolved. There are yes's that are now no's and no's that have turned into yes's. We can be who we are and be striving for something more at the same time. Values are both actual and aspirational. What we are motivated by and act on now, and what we would like to be and act on as we evolve, shape our leadership capacity. The best way to know the difference is to consider actual values as describing *why* we do what we do and aspirational values as describing *what we want to do* that we don't do consistently today.

One leader I know described her aspirational value as wanting to be someone who valued others *and* valued herself. She found that often she would put other people's needs above her own, consistently enough that it was undermining her ability to accomplish what she wanted to achieve. For her, the value she wanted to adopt was self-care, so she began taking opportunities to protect her own needs.

Another leader described himself as arrogant. His aspirational value was to be more benevolent and put the needs of others above his own. After communicating this to his team, they would caringly point out when his arrogance presented itself, and he would step back into practicing his aspirational value of putting others first. It isn't important whether values are actual or aspirational, as long as they are guiding behaviors in our desired direction.

Why Values Matter in Leadership

Most organizations have a list of core values that are displayed on the wall and show up in a variety of company marketing materials, from coffee mugs to baseball caps. During orientation, many organizations train their new hires about their values and how to live them. And yet, on any number of occasions, you can see leaders acting in direct opposition of what they claim to be their values. These are often the same companies in which, two weeks after new-hire orientation, someone takes you to lunch and explains the real values of the organization. Or, if no one is looking out for you, you find out only after stepping on a cultural land mine.

Values serve an important purpose for leaders. They provide a strategic road map for the vitally important to seemingly mundane everyday decisions. Unfortunately, not enough leaders consistently live their values through daily actions, which has a huge negative impact on teams, organizations, and communities. Consider how different the United States economy would have been in 2009 had our financial leaders been more concerned with the financial health of individuals and their families, rather than padding their own wallets. Numerous examples—from Enron to American International Group—highlight what can and does happen when leaders lack values or lack the courage to take a stand based on those values. Let's look at a more recent example. More than 5,300 Wells Fargo Bank employees opened fraudulent accounts with the intent to meet or exceed incentive plans put in place for the employees. The bank was fined more than $100 million.[5] As of this writing, little more is known about the intent of the employees or their leadership. However, this does bring into question the values of the organization and how these values drove employees to repeatedly act criminally.

According to Aubrey Malphurs, a professor at Dallas Theological Seminary and author of *Values-Driven Leadership*, a leader's behavior establishes the norm for the organization, thereby setting the tone for the organization's values. He states that "*values are the basis for all your behaviors, the bottom line for what you will or will not do*" (emphasis added). Malphurs also asserts that it's extremely important that leaders have a fundamental understanding of their own beliefs. This drives how an organization then addresses the basis of its everyday operations, rather than having the operations drive the everyday beliefs of the leader.[6]

We also know from research that we often emulate behaviors we see in others, another big reason for leading with values in the workplace. In 1992, a research team at the University of Parma, Italy, discovered in macaque monkeys a phenomenon called "mirror neurons"—cells in the brain that fired both when a monkey took an action (like eating a banana), as well as when the monkey observed an action performed by another (a man eating a banana).[7] In short, the neuron "mirrors" the behavior of the other, as though the observer were itself performing the action. More recent research indicates that humans, like monkeys, also have these mirror neurons. In 2005, the PBS television series *NOVA scienceNOW* interviewed neuroscientist Daniel Glaser of University College London, who explained that inside our heads, we are constantly "acting out" and imitating whatever activity we're observing.[8]

In fact, we sometimes even confuse our own actions with those of other people. A 2010 study from the University of Münster in Germany reported that people who had watched a video of someone else doing a simple action—such as shaking a bottle or shuffling a deck of cards—often mistakenly recalled two weeks later that they had done so themselves. More than 25 percent of participants in this study, as well as in several follow-up experiments, created "false memories" after watching someone else, even when they were warned that they might mix up other people's actions with their own.[9] Although this research in humans is still relatively new, more and more studies are making ties between what we see in others and how we behave. The result of this is that a leader who takes a stand teaches others to mirror the same kind of commitment to values in the workplace.

Clarity on Values

When we are conscious of what is important to us, our conscious and subconscious mind finds the important elements in our environment to assist us in living our values. If we determine justice is important to us, opportunities to seek justice will become more obvious, and our world will be one in which righting wrongs becomes prevalent. If we choose beauty, then our mind will find the beauty in others and in situations where others see nothing but ugliness. If we choose hard work, then our minds will find more work to do. This is called *selective attention*: the capacity for, or process of, reacting to certain stimuli selectively when several occur simultaneously. According to many bodies of research converging on selective attention theory, to some extent, our awareness of the world depends on what we choose to pay attention to, not merely on the stimuli entering our senses. Think about the number of stimuli that vie for our attention in the course of the day. Just sitting where you are now, reading this book, consider all the stimuli you have unconsciously blocked out so that you can focus on reading. If you give yourself time to focus on allowing more or different stimuli in, you'll likely begin to see or hear things you didn't before.

For example, is there a humming from your computer, or maybe the sound of a coffee maker? As I write this, I'm in my home office, and as I turn my attention to the sounds around me, I hear birds outside my window that were always there but I did not attend to.

What do you see? Is there an item on your desk that you didn't know was there before and, as you give it your attention, you realize it was there all along? If not your desk, walk out into the hall and notice the space around you. Do you notice something new?

Maybe the best example of this is when you have just bought a brand-new, shiny car that feels unique and perfect in every way, until you get on the highway and, everywhere you look, you see the exact make, model, and color of your car. Is it that those cars suddenly multiplied during the time you were making your purchase, or is it that these cars were stimuli that you did not actively attend to before as you do now?

When we are clear about what is important to us, we put our conscious *and* subconscious to work looking for the people and things around us that will support living our values.

Now comes the task of getting clear about our personal values. In some ways, our values are uniform and will reflect values that also resonate with others—integrity, respect, and dignity. There are also values that are unique to us. In addition to common values, you may value order, security, and thoughtfulness. The first step in taking a stand is to be clear about your values so that, as a leader, you know what stands are necessary to take for yourself and for others.

There are three ways to get clear about your own values: Evaluate your responses in tough times; evaluate your life choices; and evaluate your natural inclinations and talents.

Evaluate Your Responses in Tough Times

Tough times give us an opportunity to get clear about our values. After the situation with Oscar and the client, Daniel realized that, although respect for others is a value for him, he didn't activate that value when he had the chance. He was not courageous enough to take a stand. This may have been a failure, but not all is lost for Daniel. Tough times give us an opportunity for self-discovery. Our leadership values will be tested and shaped by many situations and people. Some of the toughest people in our lives are our greatest teachers. They allow us to experience the contrast of their values with our own. In the process, we learn as much about ourselves from those who contradict our values as from those with whom we comfortably aligned.

Going back to John McCain's story from "The Courage to Get Unstuck," in tough times, he was able to use the situation and time to reflect on what was most important to him. He could evaluate whether caring for his own needs was more important than taking a stand for other captive soldiers and for his country. In this way, the insight he gleaned from his captors—his tough people—helped him refine and activate his values in the most powerful way. To this day, his legacy and confidence in these values remain intact and visible in how he lives his life. From the experience of being held captive and tortured, he is one of the most well-known senators to speak out against enhanced torture tactics at Guantanamo Bay. In a moving address to the U.S. Congress, he outlined his thoughts, contrasting the behaviors of our enemies with the values of the American people. Senator McCain said, "The enemy we fight has no respect for human life or human rights. They don't deserve our sympathy. But this isn't about who they are. This is about who we are. These are the values that distinguish us from our enemies."[10]

Evaluate Your Life Story

Evaluating your life story is one of the most profound and useful activities I use with leaders in helping them identify their values. Start by creating a timeline that indicates the time you were born until now, and list in between those dates all the significant people and events that helped shape who you are as a leader today. You may want to write your story and then set it aside for a few days before coming back to it to see whether there is anything you have left out. Once you've finalized the life story on your timeline, spend some time reflecting on what you have developed. What does this story tell you about how you came to be the leader you are?

Evaluate Your Natural Inclinations and Talents

Your natural inclinations or talents are things that are as familiar to you as breathing. They are the parts of your persona that are consistent, are easily identifiable by others, and are something you usually take for granted. You can evaluate your natural inclinations by reflecting on questions that ask you to consider the things you do regularly and others have come to expect of you. Start by answering the questions below:

- What did you love to do as a kid? Why did you love to do this?
- What gets you excited to start your day?
- What would you miss the most if it were taken away from you?

- What do others look to you for?
- What was a time of real happiness for you? Why was this time important?
- Why do people reach out to you instead of someone else?
- What are you doing when you're at your best?
- If you won the lottery tomorrow, what would you *not* change about how you live your life?

After you have accomplished all three steps, review what you've learned about yourself and identify 30 words, phrases, or statements that best describe the values you identified. For example, Table 3.1 shows the top 30 value words and phrases from my own evaluation of my leadership values.

Table 3.1 Angela's Top 30 Value Words

Abundance	Enjoy	Persuade
Accomplish	Excel	Relate with God
Be accountable	Exercise	Results
Results	Family	Risk
Be spiritual	Generosity	Sensitivity
Charity	Give	Stimulate
Coach	Health	Teach
Courage	Improve	The unknown
Drive	Inspire	To feel good
Emote	Move forward	Work hard

Next, refine your list to only 10 value words, phrases, or statements. The best way to do this is to look at the 30 and identify where there may be larger, broader themes at play. To make this fun and unique to you, choose a word or create a phrase that summarizes a theme that best describes your values. For example, when I looked at my list, *be spiritual*, *relate with God*, *emote*, *health*, *family*, and *exercise* are words and phrases that describe ways in which I choose to live the spiritual part of my life. So when I reduced the value words to 10,

I created a phrase—"Live spiritually"—to represent these multiple values. Likewise, move, risk, improve, drive, and stimulate were all values that described my desire always to be evolving and growing. They also seemed to describe forward motion, so I decided to call these values "Move forward." Table 3.2 shows the 10 values that I refined from my original 30 values.

Table 3.2 Angela's 10 Distilled Value Phrases

Be accountable for my actions	Influence and inspire others
Enjoy life	Live spiritually
Express emotions	Take risks
Move forward	Teach and coach others
Give to others	Work harder

Finally, from your list of 10, refine your list once more to your top three value words, phrases, or statements. Keep in mind that in doing this you are not taking values off the list but rather prioritizing the most important values to you, as I did in Table 3.3.

Table 3.3 Angela's Three Core Values

Be accountable	Move forward	Live spiritually

Now that you have your list of core values, take a moment to consider what these values say about you. Do they describe a person who values continuity, peaceful collaboration, and security, or do they describe a risk taker who cares about the environment and living free? There are no right or wrong answers. The point is to be clear about what is important to you and to let your values be your leadership guide.

Activating Our Values

As we've already discussed, tough times are an opportunity for us to activate our core values and take a stand. Let's look at an example of a global business that demonstrates for us the way to do this well.

Citrix is a high-tech organization based in South Florida where I live. In 2014, they were named one of the Top 25 Companies for Culture and Values.[11] I spend a good amount of my time working with the leaders at Citrix, and I even had the opportunity to attend their values-driven leadership training hosted by The Arbinger Institute. In this program, leaders learn how to lead and work with integrity and respect for each other.

Toward the end of 2015, Citrix made the tough decision to reduce its workforce. There had been a lot of tension in the air for weeks leading up to the event. Many employees knew something was going on. I'd hear a little here and there about the rumors flying around, but for the most part people stayed focused on their work and did their best. When the layoffs came, few seemed surprised, and some even recounted to me how ethical and compassionate the senior leadership's approach had been during the process. One employee shared with me that her experience was as pleasant as it could be, given the circumstances. Based on the stories I heard, it appeared that the leaders took specific steps to activate their values in this tough time. Instead of shocking the organization with the announcement of layoffs, the leaders shared a message in advance that layoffs were coming and communicated a specific time the leadership would address the organization with the changes.

During the communication process, employees were treated with dignity and respect. They were given the opportunity to walk the halls and say good-bye to their colleagues rather than immediately being escorted out. Those who remained at the organization were given time to process the separation before being expected to perform again. These steps demonstrate an organization that made a conscious effort to take a stand and chose actions that aligned with its values.

Since this time over a year ago, I had a chance to talk with Donna Kimmel, Senior Vice President and Chief People Officer at Citrix. She shared with me that Citrix is heading in an exciting and vibrant direction. It has redefined its mission and vision and, as a result, built upon its values. Donna said the values are fundamental to its culture and are at the heart of what makes Citrix special. It added unity, curiosity, and courage to the critical values of integrity and respect that had gotten it to where it is today. When I asked Donna to share with me more about courage, specifically, she explained, "We are a company of talented, dedicated people who take great pride in not just *what* we do but *how* we do it. Courage, as a living value, empowers us to be bold, dream big, and contribute to the success of our customers, partners, and people." Donna went on to say they will know they've reached their goal of living their values when the words they use to describe who they are align with the words others use to describe them.

In politics, we see many opportunities to take a stand as well. After former Republican Speaker of the House John Boehner announced his resignation, Paul Ryan was almost immediately called upon to the fill the open position. Initially he turned down the opportunity to run, explaining that his children were at a vital developmental age and it was more important for him to be at home in Wisconsin with his family. After some pressure, he conceded. However, he also took a very significant stand, declaring that he would take the position only if he could return home on weekends to spend time with his family, rather than campaigning for the party, as did previous speakers of the House. He also made a specific request regarding the support of the party before agreeing to take the position. In doing so, Paul Ryan was able to make a healthy decision about his leadership role for himself, his family, and his country that was based on his values.[12]

Opportunities to take a stand present themselves in our everyday vocations and community involvement. By day my father works as an air safety investigator, but evenings and weekends he spends his time in his airplane hangar or in the air. In 2007, he built a Van's RV-7 aircraft and now flies it all over the country. Soon after, he began formation flight training, becoming qualified to fly the wingman and lead positions during airshows. One of his team's signature accomplishments was a 50-ship formation flight for a NASCAR pre-race flyover timed perfectly with the end of the National Anthem. Getting 50 airplanes in the air, bringing them together for the formation, separating the flight for landing, then landing is no small task. Given the speed and close proximity of the aircraft, flight formation team shows can be very dangerous. The lead pilot sets the pace and direction for all other pilots on the team. Rather than focusing on the path ahead, the pilots focus on the plane they are flying off of. If the leader turns or changes altitude, the other pilots simply stay in position as trained, often unaware that the flight direction or altitude has changed. Any lack of attention and focus from any of the pilots could be deadly.

After attending a local airshow with my kids, I reached out to my dad by text and asked him when he would be performing again. I wanted to take them to see their grandfather do such an amazing thing and see how he plays such an important role in leadership. But my dad responded with this text instead.

> I quit doing the air show formation stuff because I could not get a core group of pilots to practice regularly and/or be available for the air shows. I'm not popular with the group anymore. As such, I left the team. I did not want to be in a flight and someone get hurt or killed. I will start another group someday, but only with a group of dedicated pilots that can afford the commitment. You know me, I strive to be a perfectionist and get annoyed when others put forth minimal effort.

Boy, do I know about his perfectionism! As his daughter, it's what helped form my "Move forward" value that seems to haunt me every time I want to give up or stay comfortable. But for my father, leading a dangerous activity without a team committed to perfection was a risk he was not willing to take. His stand came in the form of stepping out of his leadership role and leaving the team.

Taking a stand is the most observable way to demonstrate what matters to you and to role model what you expect from others you lead. It is also one of the most painful things to do because it's usually not popular, and there is often a consequence that you'd rather avoid. But given that you know who you want to be now, and you're clear about your values, you'll know where it matters most for you to take a stand.

Chapter Application

Questions to Consider

1. Are you clear on what you stand for as a person and as a leader?
2. Are you aware of your organization's values? If so, do you believe you role model these values?
3. Are there values that you aspire to live? If so, have you considered how you plan to change your behaviors to live these values?

Strategies for Taking a Stand

1. Identify key observable behaviors associated with living these values:
   a. When people think about you, what are some values that they would immediately say you live?
   b. What specific behaviors would reflect your most treasured values?
   c. How can you emphasize these behaviors more in your life?
2. Identify situations that require you to take a stand based on these values.
3. Share these values in an observable place.
4. Share these values with others who will hold you accountable.

Notes

1. Gurteen, David. "On Excellence and Habit by Aristotle." Accessed December 1, 2016. http://www.gurteen.com/gurteen/gurteen.nsf/id/X0005FBA6/.

2. Hartup, Willard W. "Social Relationships and Their Developmental Significance." *American Psychologist* 44, no. 2 (February 1989): 120–6.

3. Hinde, Robert A. *Individuals, Relationships and Culture*. Cambridge, United Kingdom: Cambridge University Press, 1987.

4. Kohlberg, Lawrence. *Essays on Moral Development*. Vol. 2, *The Psychology of Moral Development: The Nature and Validity of Moral Stages*. New York: Harper & Row, 1984.

5. Singal, Jesse. "Why It's Unlikely Anyone Will Go to Jail Over Wells Fargo's Massive Fraud Scheme." Daily Intelligencer, *New York Magazine*, September 9, 2016. http://nymag.com/daily/intelligencer/2016/09/why-no-one-will-go-to-jail-over-wells-fargos-fraud-scheme.html.

6. Malphurs, Aubrey. *Values-Driven Leadership: Discovering and Developing Your Core Values for Ministry*. Grand Rapids, MI: Baker Books, 1996.

7. di Pellegrino, G., L. Fadiga, L. Fogassi, V. Gallese, and G. Rizzolatti. "Understanding Motor Events: A Neurophysiological Study." *Experimental Brain Research* 91 (1992): 176–80.

8. Tyson, Peter. "Monkey Do, Monkey See." *NOVA scienceNOW*, January 1, 2005. http://www.pbs.org/wgbh/nova/body/glaser-monkey.html.

9. Ehrenfeld, Temma. "Reflections on Mirror Neurons." *Observer* 24, no. 3 (March 2011). http://www.psychologicalscience.org/index.php/publications/observer/2011/march-11/reflections-on-mirror-neurons.html.

10. McCain, John. "McCain Statement on Detainee Amendments." October 5, 2005. http://www.mccain.senate.gov/public/index.cfm/speeches?ID=0effe15d-0a29-4940-b052-74206536325a.

11. "Citrix Honored as One of the Top 25 Companies for Culture and Values in 2014, a Glassdoor Employees' Choice Award." Business Wire, September 30, 2014. http://www.businesswire.com/news/home/20140930006218/en/Citrix-Honored-Top-25-Companies-Culture-Values.

12. Gilbert, Craig. "Paul Ryan Says He Would Serve as House Speaker – with Conditions." *Journal Sentinel Online* (Milwaukee, WI), October 20, 2015. http://www.jsonline.com/news/statepolitics/gop-caucus-to-take-up-house-speaker-job-paul-ryans-decision-pending-b99600016z1-334671051.html.

4 The Courage to Be Humble

Humility does not mean thinking less of yourself than of other people, nor does it mean having a low opinion of your own gifts. It means freedom from thinking about yourself...at all.[1]

—William Temple, former Archbishop of Canterbury

Jason was a rising star, a real go-getter who had moved from operational lead to branch manager to regional manager and was now being promoted to divisional president, all within the first 10 years of his career. Impressive, right? We've all known leaders like Jason. Smart, competent, quick on their feet, and influential. If you talked with Jason's customers, they would describe a resourceful and talented man who is a trusted advisor. But if you talked to anyone who worked closely with him, he or she would tell you a different story. Jason had a no-nonsense approach that often left others feeling dismissed and shut down. Jason has been known to shut a door in the face of an employee who showed up without a meeting scheduled and ignore requests to attend meetings hosted by his peers. Jason's favorite line around the office when others didn't agree with his decisions was "I hate to say it, but I am the boss," and then he flashed a coy smile. Jason was infamous for what his peers referred to as "double-talk." As one of his peers described it, Jason would tell you he supported you, then undermine you with another peer.

All of Jason's behaviors seemed to go undetected by leadership, who continued to promote him, until one day when Jason found himself squaring off with a new boss over an underperforming employee. Jason felt that his employee, Matthew, had been given too many second chances and needed to be removed from the organization. Jason's boss, Erica, didn't agree with Jason. She felt that Matthew's performance was not an issue but rather that Jason was targeting Matthew because he would appropriately stand up to Jason and communicate necessary concerns. Jason then argued to demote Matthew or at a minimum move him to another team. Erica felt it was important for Matthew to maintain his position because he had done nothing to deserve a demotion or transfer. During a team meeting a few weeks later, Jason aired his concerns about Matthew's performance, going so far as to suggest that Matthew reach out to Erica to find him a home on another team because he wasn't fitting into the culture Jason was trying to establish. Stunned, Matthew got up, left the meeting, and walked down to Erica's office.

When Erica heard what had transpired, she was also stunned. She asked Matthew to go back to his desk and told him she would investigate the situation. She called Jason into her office and asked him to explain the situation from his perspective. According to Erica, Jason said, "I appreciate your coaching but it is up to me how to manage my team, and Matthew will no longer be a part of it. If you want to hold on to baggage, you can find him a job." Erica sat in her chair, speechless.

There is a line between confidence and arrogance. And it's not a fine line, but a big, bold line, highlighted and underscored. *Confidence is the appreciation of your own needs and contributions, as well as those of others.* Confidence is not only an appropriate trait for leadership but also an essential one. *Arrogance, on the other hand, is the lack of appreciation for others' needs and contributions.* Although you don't know *this* Jason, we all know *a* Jason, and some of us have even been Jason. Using traditional terms with new definitions, we can see Jason's problem was arrogance rather than confidence. To be a leader who has the courage to be humble, we need to understand arrogance through a different lens, one that provides a new perspective and application of humility in the workplace.

Arrogance in the Workplace

Just like bad car exhaust, arrogance pumps foul smoke into the air that builds up over time. Before we know it, we are breathing in harmful toxins in a polluted work environment. Researchers from the University of Akron and Michigan State University learned that high levels of arrogance are associated with low levels of humility and agreeableness. In addition, their research revealed that high levels of arrogance significantly and negatively affected the leader's performance and ability to lead teams and create a positive culture.[2]

Here are some quick examples of how arrogance can show up and negatively affect the workplace environment:

- Team members one-upping one another rather than working together collaboratively
- Team members politicking and agenda setting rather than supporting each other's ideas
- Disrespectful undermining and passive aggressive behaviors
- Taking credit for someone else's work
- Unhealthy competition that creates silos, duplicated effort, and unnecessary failures

Intentions, Behaviors, and Arrogance

Chanda, a controller of a small private company, shared with me that recently she had been given feedback that she was showing up as arrogant. This was troublesome for her and a blind spot. She hadn't considered herself arrogant and wasn't sure what she was doing that led to this perception. I asked her to give me an example of where she found herself at odds with someone else. She described a typical scenario where someone would call to justify an investment, without really having thought through the request. She said usually the conversation would escalate and end in frustration on both ends. I asked her whether she felt her needs and contributions were more important than the people she would talk to in these situations. She said that yes, at times she felt like her contributions were greater and their contributions were less because they were less competent. I then asked her to draw a line down the center of a piece of paper and, in the left-hand column, write down the behaviors she would typically use in these scenarios. Figure 4.1 shows what she wrote.

In the right-hand column, I asked her to write down the behaviors she would use if *her intention was to consider others' needs as important as her own.* See Figure 4.2.

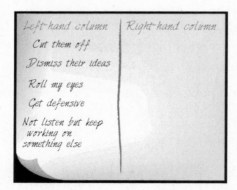

Figure 4.1 When Our Needs and Contributions Are More Important

Chanda's honest self-reflection provides a road map for better understanding intentions and behaviors. Our intention can be defined as all the things we are thinking about and planning to do that we have not yet acted on. Our nonverbal and verbal behaviors are what signal our intention to others. Because no one can really

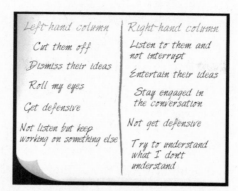

Figure 4.2 When Others' Needs and Contributions Are as Important as Our Own

know what's in our heart—what we truly believe and what we truly intend to do—others look at our behaviors to determine our character. When we truly believe others' needs are less important and their contributions less significant than our own, then our behaviors will likely mirror this intent, and others will see us as arrogant.

Let's go back to Jason's example of arrogance and look at his intention versus his behavior. Jason wanted to support his peers, but when he would say one thing and do another (double-talk), his peers coined him as arrogant. When Jason didn't agree with his boss's decision, his intention was to get the outcome he wanted. Erica saw his behavior with Matthew as retaliatory and his behavior with her as insubordinate. Both behaviors Erica found as unacceptable.

For most leaders, like Chanda, the definition of arrogance is incongruent with how they like to see themselves. Chanda did not like hearing that she was arrogant. This certainly was not how she saw herself, but she was honest when admitting that she did not always value others' contributions as much as her own. Just because it doesn't feel good to hear doesn't mean it isn't true. One of the greatest learning opportunities we have is to sit with our discomfort, rather than disarming our discomfort by rationalizing or dismissing it. By sitting with the word *arrogant* and its definition, you can examine whether it is, in fact, okay with you to be this way. If so, continue with the full acknowledgement of who you are and, if not, make strides to change.

Arrogance Is the Birthplace of the Humbling Experience

Myra leads a multimillion-dollar not-for-profit organization. When Myra and I first met, she disclosed to me her overwhelming frustration with her senior leadership team. It didn't take long to uncover that at the heart of her team's poor performance was Myra herself. At first, Myra was defensive and unwilling to accept my findings, but after a couple of days she agreed to explore the problem further. After sharing some feedback with her, I was able to help her see that how she was choosing to engage with her team was leading directly to the very problems she was insisting should stop. A little less weary of the data, she asked how this was affecting the organization. I asked her whether I could lead several skip level meetings with her to help her gain some additional insight into her question. During this process, Myra met with groups of her direct reports' team members. During these meetings, I asked questions and facilitated discussions that led to a breaking point for Myra. After only our second round of meetings, with six more to go, she asked me to stop. After everyone left, she left, too, and I didn't hear from her for two days.

Myra's experience is what I call *The Humbling Experience*. The Humbling Experience is an opportunity that arises which allows us to practice humility. For Jason, our leader from the beginning of this chapter, his Humbling Experience came in the form of a demotion and, soon after, his termination, due to his arrogance. I've seen other scenarios where a leader learned that his team was conspiring to get rid of him. They had established an elaborate plan to set him up so that others could see his faults. Needless to say, the leader was devastated.

The Humbling Experience can range from a corrective performance conversation with someone you respect to being asked to find employment somewhere else. There is no shortage of humbling experiences that can present themselves during your leadership journey. Most important, the Humbling Experience is not optional; every leader gets one. At least one. If you are attempting to personify leadership, at one point or another you will fail. You will overestimate your contributions and ignore the contributions of others. You will find yourself confused, baffled, and lost. It doesn't matter what your title is; humility does not differentiate between CEO and plant manager. No matter who you are, you will need courage to stand up again after you've been brought to your knees.

About 10 years ago, I was leading the training and development function for a multibillion-dollar construction materials company. During my tenure, I created a very successful leadership development program that had tremendous impact on the organization's results and changed the lives of many.

With my success came a ton of praise and attention. While others my age were cutting their teeth on stretch assignments, I was running a highly effective department. While my peers were vying for the attention of our CEO, I was sipping wine with him in the first-class airport lounge. It's safe to say I had lost total perspective. I was 29 years old and arrogant.

My Humbling Experience struck like a lightning bolt and felt like a punch to the gut. During the delivery of my annual leadership program, I had several leaders pull me aside to tell me they thought I was arrogant and hypocritical. They said they were concerned about the quality of their experience and requested I consider changing some of my behaviors. I was mortified. I ended up breaking down in tears (the first and only time in my career) in front of the entire leadership group. They sat there staring, dumbfounded and completely uncomfortable, while I sobbed. A few weeks later I was turned down for a global promotion that I was the only one in the running for. It goes without saying, these are not my proudest moments, and it still feels vulnerable to share them with you now. But this was the experience that broke me and got my attention. This was my Humbling Experience.

When we are arrogant, The Humbling Experience will find us. It's as if the god of our leadership evolution requires us to face the ugliness inside ourselves and challenge it to a duel. In this experience we have the opportunity to grow, mature, and find a better version of ourselves. If we don't, we are doomed to repeat the lesson.

It used to be that when I looked back on my Humbling Experience, I would do so with a wince and a whimper. But with time I could face it front and center. I can share it now with countless readers because it has no power over me. Instead, it reminds me that I am human and, therefore, imperfect. I'm a work in progress, and I'm better today than I was yesterday. I have my Humbling Experience to thank for that. Facing The Humbling Experience causes plenty of discomfort and pain. The easiest thing to do is run away, lick your wounds, and then come back as if nothing has happened. But in doing so we rob ourselves of the opportunity to practice humility.

Let's revisit my story about Myra. With a couple of days to think, Myra realized that she had an opportunity to practice humility and came back to me with a proposal. She said she wanted to restructure our meetings moving forward. During her two days away, she had outlined what she referred to as her "acknowledgments"—the things she was responsible for doing that had led to the breakdown and dysfunction of the organization. We resumed our skip level meetings, but this time Myra opened the meetings by sharing her acknowledgments with her direct reports and members of their teams. In each instance, the people in the room were visibly surprised. Some of them were stunned and quiet, while others demonstrated their shock with dropped jaws. It wasn't like Myra to admit faults and mistakes.

The Humbling Experience can and does happen to everyone, especially those seeking to grow in leadership. For the person it's happening to, like Myra and me, it feels sudden and unexpected. But for those observing, it seems obvious and even anticipated. A long list of leaders have risen and fallen in the collapse of the world economy in recent years. We've witnessed their Humbling Experiences in painfully public ways, yet there are others who unknowingly await their fate. The good news is there is something we can do for ourselves and for the leaders who work along with us. Arrogance is not a curse without an antidote; it is a choice. And like Myra, leaders have a choice about what to do with their Humbling Experience.

Why Humility Matters

Myra's team and organization didn't change overnight after those meetings, but things did change because of her humility and responsibility for her own shortcomings. When leaders like Myra embrace humility, they can expect to reap rich rewards, even if the process is painful and requires bountiful courage.

We are all capable of doing more, being more, and reaching further when we work from a place of humility. Who we aspire to be isn't about us at all but about the organization, the community, or the family we lead and to which we belong. With humility, we are more capable of:

- Doing the right thing regardless of our stake in the game
- Hearing tough messages
- Getting to the root cause of a problem
- Gaining trust and respect with those at all levels of the organization
- Delivering consistent and sustainable results
- Being authentic
- Building alliances
- Resolving conflict

Minimize Self and Maximize Our Bigger Purpose

There are two leadership paths available to us: one path that is self-seeking and one that is about seeking a bigger purpose. The distinction between these paths comes from a clear understanding of who we are, what we want to be, and what we want to give. These are not questions with answers we can fake; they are answered in the way we live our lives.

Self-Seeking

The first path is the path of least resistance and is well worn. Travelers on this path seek to serve their own needs and their own purpose. You don't have to look hard to find these kinds of leaders. They dominate our politics, they show up in our media telling us why we should listen to them, and they run rampant in every structure that houses a leader. The self-seeking path fills a void for the ego and is rooted in fear.

Carrie remembers the first time she met Jackson when he joined the company. She described him as "genuine and inspiring." She recounts that, in their first meeting, he was eager to learn what motivated her and how he could help her succeed. She left that meeting grateful that she finally had the chance to work for a strong and capable leader from whom she could learn. During the first couple of years, she did in fact grow and develop under his tutelage and so did the organization. He was not only a good coach but also a visionary. Within months he had crafted a vision for the organization's future that seemed different from anything Carrie or others had heard before. For an organization that had suffered many setbacks in a shrinking industry, he infused hope and pride back into his people, and they in turn found the capacity to do the same for their people. In a short period, Jackson had changed the culture and the profit margins for the better.

Going into Jackson's third year with the company, something seemed to change for him. He was increasingly unsettled with his success and more eager to move up the ranks. He began commenting that his boss was unable to lead at the executive level. He shared with Carrie on many occasions his desire to move into an executive role and became frustrated when the opportunity did not present itself quickly enough. He started participating in many global cross-functional teams and spearheading committees. He also found ways to lead outside of the organization, joining the board of a respectable local business and becoming an adjunct professor for a well-known university. Before Carrie knew it, her once attentive and visionary leader had become invisible. In the absence of Jackson leading the day-to-day business, Carrie and her team struggled. Debates began between peers about what direction to take on key initiatives. At first, Jackson's unavailability was just a nuisance. Because he had developed such goodwill with his people, his transgressions were initially overlooked and the business stayed steady. As time went on, though, Jackson's absence began to affect results. Carrie's once cohesive peer team began to fall apart and their profits spiraled downward.

During a meeting in which Carrie and her peers found themselves once again struggling to move forward without Jackson's direction, they agreed something had to be done. The team felt strongly that Jackson's personal ambition was outweighing what was best for the organization, and they were fed up. They agreed someone needed to share their concerns and ask Jackson to reengage. Carrie, of course, was elected.

As you might imagine, Carrie didn't sleep much the night before her scheduled meeting with Jackson. She tossed and turned, thinking about how she was going to express the team's concerns and wondering how he would respond. The next day she went to the office only to find out she had lost sleep for no reason. Jackson had been let go and was being replaced by an interim leader until the organization could find someone else for the position. Jackson's boss had flown in from headquarters to explain the situation to Jackson's team. He said that although Jackson had a great first couple of years, his lack of focus on the basics in the most recent years was creating bigger problems than the ones he was able to solve in the beginning. In other words, the pain he was causing the organization exceeded his value and worth. A once exceptional turnaround leader was now a fallen star, all because he became too ambitious. Instead of leading his business, he was busy trying to grow his own visibility and position within the organization.

Unfortunately for Jackson, the self-seeker's path is limited. Of course, he didn't see that. He could see only the corporate ladder, with his foot on one rung and his competition reaching for the rung above him. He couldn't see the bigger purpose of the ladder because he saw only himself in comparison with others. Therefore, his visibility was limited. Jackson is not the only one who suffered in this story. Jackson's team and his organization lost, too. Jackson was capable of giving much more of himself to others, but was unable to access that potential; it was locked behind his self-imposed bars of overachievement.

Seeking a Bigger Purpose

The second path is one of seeking a bigger purpose. Some leaders are lucky and are born with a disposition for the second path, but for most of us this path is harder to find and takes work to cultivate. Usually we stumble upon it after many Humbling Experiences. Travelers on this path seek to serve the needs of something bigger than themselves. They understand their role is to guide and facilitate others to see what's possible. The bigger-purpose seeker serves to create opportunity and possibility, and unlike the self-seeker fixated on climbing the corporate ladder, bigger-purpose leaders shed themselves of the need to be at any place in comparison to anyone.

Both self-seekers and bigger-purpose seekers are capable of moving people from one destination to another. The difference is their intention in doing so. The intent of bigger-purpose leaders is to reach a goal that serves others. They believe they have a gift that is intended to bring themselves and others preservation, growth, promotion, and harmony. The intent of self-seekers is to obtain these same things for themselves, but at the cost of others, if necessary.

Stephen is one of the best examples of a bigger-purpose seeker leader whom I've worked with in a long time, although my opinion of him did not start out that way. When I first met Stephen, he was both arrogant and savvy. A dangerous combination. I knew that he could convince me of anything he wanted me to believe, and I often found myself suiting up in my charisma-proof vest to dodge his wit and charm.

During a 360-degree feedback coaching session with Stephen, he learned that others did not trust him. More specifically, his peers did not trust him. Some felt Stephen was looking out only for himself and his own best interest and not necessarily working for the best interests of the team. Stephen took this feedback very seriously and over the next couple of years worked hard to gain the trust of not only his peers but also others in the organization around him.

Recently, Stephen asked me to work with him on a more extended coaching basis to identify the next step in his career. When I reunited with Stephen, I was once again suited up, but unnecessarily so. He had made the shift from self-seeker to bigger-purpose seeker. He was much more at ease with himself, giving me permission to be at ease as well. Although he was still savvy, I felt a sense of authenticity about him that I had not detected before. He was more considerate, open, and curious.

Stephen's goal was to learn how others outside of his immediate team and in other parts of the organization viewed him so that he could know what he needed to do to grow and develop. I spent several days interviewing other leaders in his organization who worked more on the periphery with Stephen. I learned that others viewed

Stephen as a rock star and more than capable of leading at the next level. Many of the more senior leaders I spoke with were adamant that Stephen needed to be aggressive and seek a new role that gave him more visibility so that he would be considered for advancement when the opportunity came up.

This feedback led Stephen down a path of seeking opportunities where he could lead more strategically, with a larger scope and more visibility. It didn't take long before an opportunity opened up for Stephen. The new position reported to Liz, a manager whom Stephen knew well. He also knew the team he would be inheriting. The new role would be a stretch, but he felt capable. In theory, this was a perfect fit, but unfortunately, it wasn't quite that simple. The only way this could be a win for Stephen was if he maintained his current team *and* took on the new team. It meant having two bosses in different areas of the organization. He would need a new structure to reflect his role as leading both groups for him to gain any real visibility. Otherwise, no one outside of his department would know Stephen's role had expanded, and his opportunity for additional visibility would diminish. But getting his current manager and Liz to agree to share Stephen in order to create a career advantage for Stephen did not seem likely. Especially when Liz would be losing some of her own visibility and scope in giving Stephen more. This, of course, made her nervous about the implications it had on her and her career. Stephen knew that, although he was the best candidate, it would be difficult if not impossible to formally create a structure that allowed for the goals of the position, Liz's goals, and his career growth to align. There was one easy option. He could take on the additional work without formalizing the structure. That would make everyone happy but undermine his longer-term goal. He was in a quandary: do what was best for his growth or do what was best for others and the organization with little benefit for him.

I found out shortly thereafter, in a conversation with Liz, that Stephen had asked to take the position with no formal changes to the structure. She said he approached her and said, "Let's just do this. It's the best thing for the organization." And like that, Stephen took on an additional team with no visible benefit to himself. He did what was best for others.

To become a bigger-purpose seeker, you have to get in touch with that part of you that believes in something bigger than yourself, that knows no matter what you may see on the surface, nothing is done in a vacuum and nothing is solely about you. Many great women and men have forged the road before you and they will continue after you. You are but one contributing thread in a magnificent and monumental tapestry hung for all the world to see. No one human is capable of this kind of achievement alone. If you can shift your thinking in this way, then you can shift your path. The best tool for making this shift is, of course, humility. Ironically, the more we experience humility, the more we reconcile the part of us that needs evidence that we are important with the part of us that already knows it. Anyone who has been in the presence of this kind of leadership knows it. You feel humbled and in complete awe.

Loving Something More Than Yourself

A few years ago, we took our two children to Disney World for the first time. At one point during the day, I found myself totally immersed in this magical experience and completely baffled that someone as serious and unchild-like as I could arrive at such a state. The landscaping was a mystical combination of color and fragrances, the characters were everywhere among us, around us, and on stage performing simultaneously. The lights and sounds all seemed to mirror the magical party that every child and adult alike was engaged in. From Donald Duck to the street cleaner, not a single employee was out of step. At one point, I turned to my husband and said, "It's as if 10,000 employees are working together in complete unison to pull off a completely flawless performance." I imagined this was exactly what Walt Disney had in mind when he originally envisioned his park. Disney was a bigger-purpose seeker who leveraged thousands of brilliant minds and childlike hearts to create something bigger than himself for all the world to love and enjoy. Walt Disney alone could not create Disney, and he was humble enough to know that. Otherwise his vision would never have come alive and left a family of four eager to return when our day ended.

Walt Disney isn't the only leadership guru who knows about the bigger-purpose seeker. Early on in my career, I had the opportunity to meet researcher and author Jim Collins. Although Collins is known for many accomplishments, his work in *Good to Great* is a leadership staple. In this book, Collins and his research team looked at the distinguishing factors among companies that went from *good* to *great*. They compared many tangible and measurable qualities of an organization's life, including its financial reporting. During the research process, Collins's team kept bringing him information about the leadership of these organizations, and Collins continued to reject it, saying he didn't want to focus on the leadership. Finally, the team was persuasive and so were their findings. In his book, he reveals the common characteristics of "Level 5 leaders" and, without much surprise, humility is a cornerstone trait for CEOs in good-to-great companies. Collins defines Level 5 leadership as "executives who build enduring greatness through a paradoxical blend of personal humility and professional will."[3]

During a flight from Boston to Denver, I happened to notice a man sitting across the aisle from me with the book *Good to Great* in his hands. He kept looking over at me, smiling. I thought it was kind of odd, so I avoided eye contact with him. But he was relentless. Finally, I stopped what I was doing and smiled back. He took this as an invitation to talk and so we began a conversation. He shared with me that while he was waiting for the flight, Jim Collins gave him his book and signed it for him. He asked me whether I knew who Jim Collins was and I answered that, of course, I did. I was then, and continue to be, someone who geeks out at the latest leadership book like a techie who geeks out at new gadgets. The gentleman told me the story of meeting Mr. Collins at the airport and all the things they talked about. I was trying not to salivate with jealousy as he talked. I asked him a ton of questions, and he gladly answered them until I came to a few he couldn't answer. Then he said, "You know, you should just ask him yourself when he wakes up." He nodded to the man slumped over asleep against the window seat next to me. My jaw dropped. Sitting next to me was Jim Collins and I hadn't even known it.

The next several minutes were a quandary for me because Collins was still asleep, and we were starting to descend. I had so many questions to ask him, but I didn't want to be rude. I was completely unaware of the "traveling next to one of your favorite best-selling authors protocol," if there was one. Luckily, he woke up as we were landing. I waited for him to gather himself before I leaned over and introduced myself. I told him I was a student of his work and asked him whether I could ask a few questions. He was extremely polite and answered, "Of course. Call me Jim." I had a list of questions, but the one thing I wanted to know the most was about leadership. So I asked him to tell me how to become a Level 5 leader. I listened and asked clarifying questions, and then, as soon as we landed, I thanked him for his time. As everyone else was departing the plane, I took out my notebook and wrote feverishly so that I wouldn't forget a word he said. His response:

> Not everyone will become a Level 5 leader, but most people can; it is more a matter of choice and discipline than a temperament. The key is to find something that you care so much about to channel yourself into, even sacrifice yourself for. We can't all be Level 5 at all things. For me, I've learned first to be Level 5 for my marriage.

I believe that being a bigger-purpose seeker means loving your purpose more than you love yourself. When you love your purpose more than you love yourself, you free yourself of the ego's need to be the center of attention. And when the ego is freed, what gets put at the center are all the things that are most important for the organizations, communities, and countries you lead.

Chapter Application

Questions to Consider

1. Do you consider yourself a self-seeker or a bigger-purpose seeker? How do you know?
2. When was the last Humbling Experience you had? How did you turn it into a learning experience?
3. What impact or benefit have you found in humility in the workplace?
4. What do you love more than yourself?

Strategies for Diminishing Arrogance

1. Identify ways to acknowledge the contributions of others that feel genuine to acknowledge.
2. Instead of using words such as *I*, *me*, and *my*, use words such as *us*, *we*, and *our* to describe accomplishments and contributions to success.
3. Give up the need to be right. The next time someone challenges you with a differing opinion, thank him or her for presenting a new perspective, and ask for time to consider the ideas. Take 24 hours to really consider his or her perspective, not as right or wrong in comparison to your ideas, but consider his or her perspective and why he or she might see things differently than you do.
4. Consider using clarifying and confirming questions to better explore others' perspectives.

Strategies for Leveraging Humility as a Learning Experience

1. Seek coaching, guidance, and support from others before trying to make sense of your experience. If you do not

allow yourself to deal with the emotions of your Humbling Experience properly first, you'll move to reaction instead of action.

2. Take time to reflect on your Humbling Experience. Look back at the behaviors over time that could have contributed to the experience and the relationships and situations surrounding it.

3. Resist the temptation to fall victim to your Humbling Experience. Instead, identify areas where, if faced with similar situations again, you could act differently.

4. Expect that humiliation will show up as part of learning and growth. Rather than seeing it as failure, see it as an opportunity to keep your ego in check and practice being a bigger-purpose seeker.

Notes

1. "William Temple Quotes." Accessed December 1, 2016. http://christian-quotes.ochristian.com/William-Temple-Quotes/.

2. Silverman, Stanley. "Identifying the Arrogant Boss." University of Akron University Communications and Marketing. July 7, 2012. http://www.uakron.edu/im/news/identifying-the-arrogant-boss/.

3. Collins, Jim. *Good to Great: Why Some Companies Make the Leap ... and Others Don't.* New York: HarperBusiness, 2001.

5 The Courage to Be Confident

Imagine if birds only sang when heard. If musicians only played when approved of. If poets only spoke when understood.[1]

—Mark Nepo, *The Book of Awakening*

Kellie was a first-time manager who, like many, was just trying to figure it all out. She loved her company, her team, and most of all, the work she did. Kellie was known by others for her contagious combination of positivity and a willingness to collaborate. When I first started working with Kellie, she was in the beginning stages of creating boundaries with others and learning to delegate. Because she was so willing to help others, at times she would struggle with saying yes, when in reality she wasn't prepared to take on the additional work and even when she really wanted to say no. To make matters worse, she had a very challenging employee who was making her rethink her decision to become a leader.

During a conversation in which Kellie was sharing some of her frustrations with the challenging employee, I said to her, "Kellie, leading people is hard. We all feel this way at times. It's not just you." Her eyes watered up and, on the verge of tears rolling down her face, she brushed them away and exhaled relief. Kellie needed validation that what she was experiencing didn't mean that she was incompetent or incapable, even though she may have been feeling that way.

Fast-forward a few years later, Kellie and I met to catch up on her development goals. This time, though, our conversation was dramatically different from the one that had ended close to tears. Kellie was comfortable, relaxed, and above all else, confident.

As we discussed some of those early conversations, and in particular, her challenging employee, we shared a lighthearted laugh. She said, "You know, as difficult as that was, it was a great learning experience. I remember not being sure if I wanted to lead or confident that I could, and now I can't imagine it any other way."

In a few short years, Kellie has gone from struggling as a new manager to truly standing out as a senior leader in her organization. She leads a strong, healthy team, and is currently working alongside her new CEO as a thought leader and partner for a major organizational change project. What a difference the courage to be confident and a little time can make.

Those People Complex

Countless leaders I've come in contact with over the years have struggled with the courage to be confident. And just like Kellie, when they struggle they wonder if maybe they are not up for the challenge of leadership. The truth is, maybe they're not. Not all people are willing to give leadership what it takes. It's a powerful role with a formidable list of responsibilities, including being able to stay strong and confident in the face of pushback. In leadership, you have to believe in yourself even when others don't. For some leaders, believing in others seems to be much easier than believing in themselves. When things go south, as they invariably do, they blame themselves rather than assessing the full picture. Unlike those who struggle to be humble, those who struggle to be confident make themselves wrong and others right. They see all the reasons why others are better and more capable and why success and happiness belong only to them. In this way, they swing too far on the pendulum past humility to a lack of ability to see and value their own strengths and contributions.

Those who lack the courage to be confident suffer from what I call Those People Complex. Those People Complex is when you see something in others that you are unwilling or unable to see in yourself. As a result, you limit your own potential. Those people—those who have what you want—they are somehow different, special, unique, or gifted in a way you are not, which therefore explains away your inability to accomplish what you want. But here is the myth buster for the Those People Complex: Every one of us has the ability to have the life we want. There is no limit to our possibilities if we choose to see ourselves as capable and worthy. I will admit, some of us want to be things that for reasons out of our control we cannot become. Maybe you wanted to join the Navy SEALs but couldn't because you are color-blind; maybe you wanted to be a baseball star but only made it to the minors due to a bad arm. Heck, I wanted to be a teenage actress and marry Kirk Cameron, but my parents were completely unwilling to take me to LA to start an acting career at age 13. For shame. But in most cases, concerning what we are here to give to the world, the real talents we have to offer, we are the only ones who limit our potential.

Growing up in a lower-middle-class family with a B-minus average and no real athletic abilities to speak of, I found myself suffering from Those People Complex. There was nothing really special about me that seemed to surface during my first 18 years on Earth. I wasn't funny, I wasn't overly smart, and I didn't have a clue how to fit in. It was hard to believe there was something exceptional about me that was yet to be revealed. It seemed there were people everywhere who had more of something I wanted, yet I was limited to what was easily accessible to me. My dad, from whom I took most of my direction, didn't always help with my lack of self-confidence. The talents I *did* have did not match what he valued. He was a technician and engineer. I was a sensitive and expressive kid. He was stable and reliable. I was a risk taker and challenging. When it came time to go to college, he filled out my college application papers and said, "Sign your name, you're going to college." The paperwork required a chosen degree so he selected it for me—early childhood education. At the time, I wanted to be a preacher, an actress, or a business owner—possibly all three. But my dad had a different idea. He said there would always be work for an elementary school teacher. I know my dad meant well, and in retrospect I can see that what he wanted for me was stability and security, which mirrored his core values. However, the message I heard was "You're not one of those people; you're not talented enough to do something more."

For the record, I believe being an elementary school teacher is an exceptionally difficult job—one that doesn't pay nearly enough and provides too little recognition for an amazing responsibility. I look at my kids' teachers all the time and I'm in awe. I am so grateful for their patience and dedication. The vocation is not the point; determining our own potential is the point. Anytime someone else selects something for us because he or she believes it's what we *should* do, and it isn't what we want for ourselves, it requires a great deal of courage to say "No thank you" and go down another path.

For me, it was only two months into my first semester that I figured out I wasn't meant to be an elementary school teacher. During a field trip to a local school, five-year-olds covered in Elmer's Glue and glitter made macaroni necklaces for the visiting college students and sang us songs. Although the necklace was heartwarming, the visit did not have the desired impact my dad would have liked. Back on campus, I walked straight back into the registrar's office and changed my major to communications without a single clue what I would do with the degree when I earned it. I won't mention in print what my dad had to say about that.

Confidence Comes from Self-Trust

Stacy and I first met when I began working with her team. After working with Stacy and observing the dynamic between her and her boss, I suggested I facilitate a conversation between the two of them. She was struggling with being able to share her concerns with him without feeling dismissed. She shared that often she would feel something was going wrong, or she would disagree with her boss, usually resulting in her losing her voice and acquiescing. For example, he had provided feedback that he valued her ability to bring out the best in her peers when they were disagreeing, and he wanted to see her step up more and help solve their problems. Instantly, she knew this was not a role she wanted to play on the team. Rather than say it, she sat quietly and let him continue talking. After the discussion, she felt sick to her stomach and wanted to find the quickest way out of the building. She wanted to tell her boss what she was feeling, but she lacked the courage.

I asked Stacy to share with me other ways she struggled with courage. She told me that her team members often commented they liked working for her because it was more like working for a peer than a manager. Secretly, she knew this wasn't really a compliment. What they were really saying is that she was not able to articulate a direction and hold them accountable to their performance. Instead, her role was more of a coach who provided feedback, offered suggestions, and was available for them to bounce around ideas. Although that was constructive, she recognized she wasn't very good at making requests of them and securing their commitments. Even when she was able to get a commitment, Stacy was very uncomfortable following up and holding them accountable.

When I asked Stacy what prevented her from saying what she wants to say and holding others accountable, surprisingly, she didn't tell me that she didn't know *how* to do it; rather, she expressed that she didn't feel qualified. Who was she to provide direction? Who was she to tell someone to do something different or provide a different perspective? The words would dance in her head but get caught in her throat before she could give power to them. Stacy struggled with what so many leaders struggle with—the ability to trust themselves, their opinions, and their beliefs. They don't trust that their voices are significant and worthy enough to be heard.

What you don't know about Stacy is that she started out as a data analyst with no experience in her field. She was a self-taught technical expert. When her department grew and needed to create a level of middle leadership, its employees recognized Stacy as someone who was not only competent but also influential and strategic. She was selected to lead her team over several other internal candidates, as well as a number of external contenders. When I met her, she had been leading her team for over seven years, hardly a new manager. During those years, she had decreased inefficiencies and cost and had increased her department's visibility as a resource to the organization. Although Stacy did not feel proficient or qualified, the data reflected otherwise.

Stacy's story is not uncommon. Raul is a software implementation team leader who is largely known for his approachability, integrity, and ability to problem solve. His team members look to him to share his insights and provide direction, but he struggles with being able to meet this need for them. One of Raul's team members described that, in the absence of his direction, the team suffers from a void of information and has difficulty making decisions. But because they respect Raul so much, they would never go around him or find another way to a solution. So they wait for direction that does not come. A deadline gets missed, a ball gets dropped, and a client is disappointed. In the midst of this, Raul knows he could have prevented it. As Raul's team struggles, it only reinforces his perception of himself as a poor leader (see Figure 5.1).

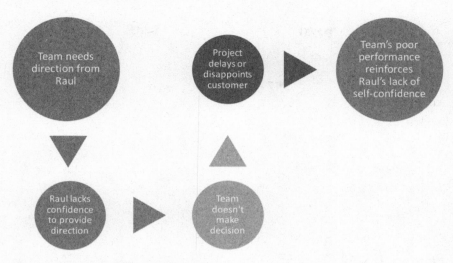

Figure 5.1 Raul's Team Struggle

Raul's team results are not the only circumstances affected by
his unwillingness to provide insight and direction. It also affects his
overall credibility and image as a leader. When he finds himself in
these situations, his most resourceful answer to this quandary is to go
to his boss. Because his boss is a command-and-control-style leader,
when faced with a problem to solve, she responds quickly and defini-
tively with an answer. Others see this as well, and as a result, instead
of seeing Raul as a leader who provides insight and direction, he is
seen as overly dependent on his boss and unable to stand on his own.
As Raul's credibility weakens with others, it only further reinforces his
perception of himself as not able to make good decisions and provide
direction (see Figure 5.2).

Over time, you can see that a leader's struggle with confidence
becomes a self-fulfilling prophecy. These leaders take less and less
risk and rely more and more on others, rather than learning to
trust themselves. "I am not capable, and therefore I don't"; "I don't
because I am not capable"; and so on. Breaking out of this cycle
requires the courage to be confident. It's a choice to do something

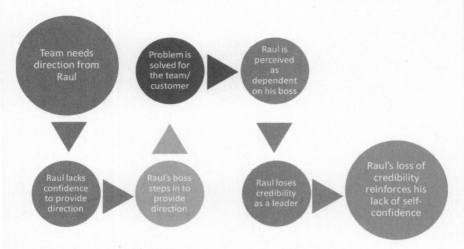

Figure 5.2 Raul's Boss Steps In

different in the face of failure. It's also a choice to believe in yourself no matter what the outcome.

Your Vote Counts, and You Get to Vote for You!

In leadership, we talk a lot about earning the trust of others. At Personify Leadership, we have developed an entire module dedicated to "The Heart of a Leader," with the intent of teaching leaders how to build trust with the people they lead. There are whole bodies of work centered solely on building other people's trust. One of my favorites is Stephen M. R. Covey's work about the Speed of Trust.[2] And yet, in leadership, we rarely dedicate resources to assist leaders in learning to trust themselves. Ironically, without self-trust and our own vote of confidence, we are likely to lose others' trust, as we saw with Stacy and Raul. These two leaders were at a place where they were unable to see themselves as worthy of their own trust. They didn't see themselves as worthy of their own vote of confidence.

Each spring, our neighborhood gets together for a chili cook-off. There are numerous entries, and all of them are good. Our family had submitted chili entries in the past, acknowledging that our entry was just for fun. We knew we were not worthy opponents. However, one year, that all changed. My husband decided to add a special ingredient, one that could transform any ordinary dish to an exceptional one. Bacon. The whole family agreed, our chili was simply amazing, and we thought for sure we had a chance to win.

When we arrived at the neighborhood park, my husband headed off to socialize, my son went to play ball, and my daughter grabbed my hand to start testing chili. We were given three plastic chips and told that we were allowed to vote for three of our favorite chilies—or put all three chips in one if we so desired. I went directly to our chili (Entry #12) and started to put my chips in the container. My daughter stopped me and said, "Mom, we can't vote for our own chili, that wouldn't be right."

I stopped for a second and considered her point. I asked her, "Cate, why do you think it's not okay to vote for your own chili?"

She responded, "Because we made it, only other people can vote for us." I told her that, in fact, was not true, and she could vote for own chili if she wanted to. She was still a little tentative, and then she said, "Okay, how about this, Mom? We are going to taste all the chilies and if we still think ours is the best, then we'll vote for our own." I thought that sounded more than reasonable, so I agreed and off we went testing over 20 chilies. When we were done we met back up at the end of the cook-off table, and she said, "Well, Mom, I hate to say it, but our chili isn't the best. I have to give my chips to #10 and #4." I smiled and agreed. I had given mine to #10 and #7.

Now, had our chili actually been the best, it would have been a shame to give up our collective six chips to a competitor we did not genuinely believe had better chili. What kind of sense does that make? No one likes a sympathy trophy, and no one should have to lose when he or she has met the winning criteria. Do you think the presidential candidates go to the ballot box and check the name of the other nominee? No way. Not only does our vote count, but we also get to vote for ourselves. If you've evaluated fairly and you still think you're the best candidate, then go ahead; do it. Vote for yourself! If *you* don't vote for yourself, how can you expect others to give you their vote of confidence?

Confidence in the Workplace

Lucas found himself in a relatively common situation. He had multiple underperformers who were affecting the overall morale and results of the team and organization. A couple in particular were very popular with the other team members and customers, not because of their performance but because of their friendly and collaborative personalities. They were so likable that it was difficult for Lucas to address performance issues directly with them out of fear of making them feel bad or of being seen as the bad guy with others.

Lucas's boss expected him to handle the team's performance. He agreed not to interfere with Lucas's decisions. Whatever he felt was necessary to improve the team's performance was up to him. In some ways, although Lucas's boss trusted him to make the right decisions for the team, Lucas wished his boss would tell him what to do, and then he would be the bad guy. Ultimately though, Lucas knew this was an opportunity to trust himself and do what was best for the team and the organization. He addressed the performance issues with his team members. Over time when improvements did not come, he made the decision to let two of the team members go, including one of the very likeable employees.

When Lucas and I talked about his choice to move forward with the team changes, he shared with me some of what he was thinking at the time. Right before communicating his decision, he almost changed his mind. He thought about all the good things the two employees had done over the years and questioned his rationale for letting them go. He then stopped and reminded himself of the reasons he had made his decision in the first place. He said he knew he had to trust he had made the right decision and move forward rather than question himself.

Not long after the underperforming employees were let go, Lucas received feedback from the remaining team about how much they respected him for making a tough decision that was in the best interests of the team. Lucas described this as a very validating experience.

Unfortunately, trusting yourself and your own judgment do not always end with a validating experience. Take Alan, for example, who was known as the golden boy of his division, a growing new revenue stream for an oil and gas company. Alan had already mastered the paradoxical combination of humility and confidence. When his peers sought his guidance, he would confidently share his winning insights but would in return ask for their guidance as well. When his senior leaders praised him for excellent work, he accepted their praise but also cautioned them the business was cyclical and things would change in time.

Sure enough, after a couple of years, the market demands did change, and his division was no longer bringing in large revenue numbers. It wasn't long before Alan's days of unbridled respect and admiration ended. After a period of intermittent communication, I e-mailed Alan to check in, and this is what he shared with me.

> I'm no longer the Golden Boy around here. I've fallen from my pedestal. I knew that things would eventually change. I know this business and I knew there would be a time when the pendulum would swing the other direction. But no one listened to me. I just have to have confidence in myself right now and know I've done the right things.

A few months after receiving this message, I found out from a mutual friend that Alan was no longer with his company.

The unfortunate thing about leadership is there are going to be times when you don't get it right or when others expected more from you, even when you attempted to appropriately modify their expectations. These are the times when you need the courage to be confident—the courage to believe in yourself and your decisions even when others don't. This doesn't mean you don't have a responsibility to reflect and learn from the situation, but there is no need to wallow in self-pity or beat yourself up. This is the time to ask yourself, "How can I learn from this situation?" and move on.

If we go back and look at the situation with Marcus in "The Business Case for Courage," we see that Marcus was confident enough to address his boss's fraudulent behaviors, he did the right thing, and he was rewarded. However, had Marcus been disciplined or let go from the organization, his decision would still have been the right thing to do. A change in outcome would not make him wrong. Courageous leaders are willing to accept that being courageous does not always produce desired outcomes.

Strategies and Tools for Building Confidence

You can lead others only if you know the way or have the confidence in yourself to find the way. Unfortunately, the path to success is usually a bit unclear, therefore requiring the latter. That makes developing the courage to be confident a survival skill in leadership. Here are some strategies for building self-confidence:

Do What You Fear the Most

One surefire way to build confidence is to do the thing you fear the most. If you survive it, and you will, assuming it's not a life-threatening act (and no, giving a presentation in front of your peers is not life-threatening), you will survive it and grow confidence from doing it. When my son was barely three years old, we had a swim instructor come to our house to teach him how to swim. The first day he was excited, but that lasted only about 2 minutes until the instructor dumped him in the water and he came up crying. He screamed for

30 minutes, the entire time of the lesson. Day two was even more painful. When the swim instructor arrived, my son saw her and ran crying into the other room. I chased him down and carried him kicking and screaming into the pool. Day three and four were pretty much the same.

But on day five something in him changed. He had resigned himself to the pain of swimming. He picked up his towel and headed to the pool when he saw the instructor coming toward the house. He headed outside without a word.

The instructor began as she normally did with small drills, and then she said, "Okay, Will, today you're going to do it. You're going to swim across the pool by yourself." I could see fear in his face, but this time he didn't fight the instructor; he just took off. He splashed his away across the pool, and I went to the other side to meet him. I picked him up out of the water and gave him a big hug.

I said, "William, that was wonderful! You swam all the way across the pool by yourself. What was that like?"

He looked up at me with a big smile, and he said, "Scary...but amazing!" Most amazing things start out scary. What do you fear the most that you wish you had the courage to do?

Appreciate Yourself More

Maleka was the vice president of marketing for a healthcare organization. She was struggling with leading her team of marketing directors at the various facilities. I had the opportunity to participate in one of her team's conference calls. When Maleka dialed in, she was not the first on the call; several of the other team members were already on the call and deep into the agenda—even though Maleka had joined several minutes before the call began. When she announced her presence, the team did not adequately acknowledge her. After a few minutes Maleka tried to engage in the conversation, but the others dominated the discussion. Toward the end, Maleka began to take the lead just as a few team members announced they had to drop off early.

This call told me a lot about Maleka and her relationship with her team. They did not appreciate her to the extent they should. Maleka was more than suited for her role. With confidence, Maleka could lead this team more effectively, leveraging their strengths and exposing some of hers. But that wouldn't happen as long as Maleka wasn't able to appreciate herself and expect others to appreciate her as well. I asked Maleka to write a letter to herself, expressing all the things she really appreciated—from her personality to her accomplishments to her life choices, and so on. My instruction was to write the letter first and then read it to at least one person she felt she could trust to be open with her, and then plan to read it to me in our next call.

This was an exercise Maleka dug into with vigor. Within a week she had called me back to read her letter to me. In it, she described a loving parent and wife, an individual with strong character and integrity, and a lifetime career in health care with a series of accomplishments and accolades. After she read the letter to me, I asked her to describe how writing this letter helped change her self-perception. She said it gave her a deeper appreciation for her strengths and contributions and made her feel more confident about authentically being who she was and not changing to fit someone else's criteria for success.

Visualize Success

When I was in high school, I was a cheerleader; however, I struggled with being able to stick a liberty—a fundamental skill for flyers. For those of you who don't know what a liberty or a flyer is, let me start by describing the basics of stunts in cheerleading. The base is the person who holds another in the air or throws and catches the person in the air. The flyer is the person whom the base holds or throws and catches. I was a flyer.

One year, our team qualified for the state championships and traveled to Orlando, Florida, for the competition. This was a huge

The Courage to Be Confident

accomplishment for a group of Midwestern kids. The only problem was that being able to stick my liberty was essential. This meant that the base would have to throw me in the air above his head, and I would have to land in his cupped hands with one foot and stay there without swaying from side to side or falling. The laws of inertia alone make this a challenging feat, and I was struggling.

The school had hired a coach to assist us with our routine, giving us the best chance to make our school proud at our first ever cheerleading competition. The coach noticed I was struggling and, after multiple failed attempts, encouraged me to consider visualizing myself hitting the stunt and sticking it over and over. She sent me home with the assignment to find a quiet corner and do nothing but visualize 15 minutes before every practice. I followed her instructions, and believe it or not, it worked. And it worked very quickly. My ability to see myself doing something with success significantly and quickly changed my ability to actually do what I was unable to do previously.

According to brain imagery research, visualization works because the neurons in our brain responsible for relaying messages to the nervous system to the body interpret mental imagery as real-life action.[3] It makes sense, then, that our ability to visualize something in our minds is an active part of being able to create a physical end result.

Act as If

Now that you've visualized what you want to do, act as if it is so without any further effort or request. For example, you may want to be the vice president (VP) of your division. Great! How would a VP in this organization act? How would the VP speak? How would the VP dress? How would the VP think? How would the VP address problems? How would the VP lead? Get clear about this visual and see yourself as this VP moving from one part of your day to another. Now, act as if you are the VP. Don't get me wrong, I'm not suggesting you jump protocol and act out of rank; just begin practicing the behaviors associated with being the person you want to be. What we learned in geometry holds true here—the shortest distance between two points is a straight line. Cut out the zigzagging path in between by acting in direct alignment with your end goal.

Establish Boundaries

Xian is a leader at a well-known small-town employer. During an off-site strategy-planning meeting, she, her boss, and her peers outlined a detailed plan for accomplishing multiple goals for that year. Xian and her peers agreed the next step would be to meet again to finalize the work they had done during this meeting. To coordinate this, her boss asked them all to book an upcoming date in their calendars. When Xian looked at her calendar, she realized this was a vacation day she had scheduled to take her son to visit colleges. She told her boss this in the hope she would understand. Unfortunately, her boss responded with "If this is important to you, then you'll change your plans."

The room got quiet and everyone waited to see how Xian would respond. She politely said, "This is very important to me, but so is the commitment I've made to my son. Can we first see if there are other dates that we can all meet before I cancel on my son?"

Xian's peers jumped at the chance to change the time, offering multiple additional dates they were available in support of Xian. They were able to agree to a new time and continue their work, and Xian was able to keep her plans in place.

If Xian had agreed to her boss's request without asking for another date option, she would have been sending the message that she is okay allowing her boss to set her set priorities for her. But because Xian was courageous enough to say something about her wishes, she established a boundary with her boss about work–life balance.

It doesn't mean Xian will never have to make personal sacrifices for work, but it does mean she has established she is willing to vocalize her needs and establish boundaries when she feels they are important.

Stop Asking for Permission

Recently, a client shared a story with me about a situation with a peer. The peer was unclear on whether to move forward on a decision because she had not involved their boss, while my client was comfortable that they could move forward without him. He told her, "Let's not delay this process. We know enough about our boss to know he'd support this decision. At least, he's never given us a reason to think this is something he needs to approve." The peer was so resistant that my client agreed, but he was not at all surprised when the boss responded, "Why are you asking me?"

It's not always easy to know your boundaries, but often those who struggle with confidence will not empower themselves when they have the opportunity. If you tend to ask for permission rather than taking an educated and empowered stand, this could be a great place to start. Everyday opportunities will present themselves to do something different. You may be surprised at how infrequently you'll actually have to say "I'm sorry" for overstepping your boundaries and how often people will view you as having exercised good judgment and timely decision-making.

Be Altruistic Without Self-Sabotage

There is an increasing awareness that altruism is a necessary skill for success in the workplace. In his book *Give and Take: A Revolutionary Approach to Success*, Professor Adam Grant from The Wharton School of business gives us some helpful language to understand how altruism (and the opposite of altruism) shows up in behaviors. He describes *Givers* as those who give the most to others, *Takers* as people who take the most from others, and *Matchers* as individuals who try to match their contributions to others' contributions.[4] Like most people, I'd much prefer an altruistic environment with more Givers and Matchers than Takers. When all of us give more, we create a culture that promotes a bigger-purpose seeker culture. When we all seek to win on behalf of the organization, there is little room for undermining success. Having said that, it's also important not to overdo altruism to the point it becomes self-sabotaging, in other words, helping others to the point of hurting ourselves. Self-sabotage occurs when we consistently make other people's needs more important than our own. In the workplace, we witness this when leaders accept consequences for their teams without asking team members to bear collective responsibility equally. Likewise, it can emerge when we consistently give others credit for our work rather than acknowledging our own contributions. Self-sabotage also occurs when we fail to ask for what we need, and instead, use our political capital to meet the needs of others. All of these are examples of thoughtful and considerate acts that are noteworthy and valuable. However, when we choose these behaviors consistently at the cost of meeting our own needs, altruism becomes a problem.

For example, take Joel, who is the support and backbone for his team. He reports directly to the senior vice president, Tamara, and advises her on all kinds of matters. He is resourceful, quick to find solutions, and capable of leveraging a diverse skill set to accomplish whatever challenge comes up for this team. Joel has his sights set on a leadership role outside of the team. He has applied many times for promotions, but has been turned down on each occasion. He receives little feedback but what he does get suggest that he needs more experience. The truth is that Joel is very experienced and qualified for most of the openings, but his title in his current role and his level in the organization do not reflect this. Joel is one of those rare team members who will do whatever is required and more, always taking on new responsibilities bigger than his job description. As a result, his position doesn't necessarily reflect his qualifications. It doesn't help matters much that his boss will give the team credit for Joel's work without specifically giving Joel praise. Joel gives to the team and Tamara without hesitation, but he doesn't claim his own contributions and grow in his career. The solution isn't to minimize giving to others but to give to yourself as well. Your needs are just as important as those of others on the team and in the organization. An appropriate level of self-promotion is a form of self-care and is essential to developing and maintaining confidence.

Developing the courage to be confident isn't something that happens overnight, but over time. A transition occurs as leaders choose to dissolve Those-People-Complex thinking and transition to self-trust and confidence. This transition requires focus and effort like any work in progress.

For me, Those People Complex has never really gone away but rather has diminished gradually over time. There are still people and situations that intimidate me, but what I choose to do in these times has changed. Instead of assuming fabricated limitations and letting opportunities pass me by, these are the times when I push myself the hardest to move to action. And trust me: it can be terribly painful. As I was first developing my confidence for these intimidating situations, I would put on a suit of armor, inhale confidence and exhale fears, lower my helmet, and raise my sword, preparing for what felt like battle. I've learned to trust myself more by doing the tough stuff and seeing that it hasn't killed me. In some cases, I've even surprised myself with the outcome. For the most part now, staying focused and continuing to be courageous, I've got the hang of it. I leave the suit of armor at home and instead put on a nice dress and Calvin Klein heels. They're way more comfortable.

Chapter Application

Questions to Consider

1. Have you found yourself struggling with the Those People Complex? If so, what are the situations or people you tend to feel this with the most?
2. Do you find it difficult to vote for yourself? If so, what is it about voting for yourself that you struggle with?

(continued)

(continued)

3. What is the thing you fear most? If you were to do it, how would it change your life for the better?

4. Do you have a vision for your success? If you are successful in achieving your goals, what will you be able to do that you can't do right now? Can you visualize yourself doing it?

5. Do you feel you have well-established boundaries? If not, what do you need to communicate to others about your priorities and needs?

6. Do you tend to ask for permission rather than empowering yourself to take action? If so, what is holding you back from taking action?

Strategies to Practice

1. Write a letter to yourself outlining all the things you appreciate about yourself. Share it with at least two people you trust.

2. Pick something that scares you and do it! Document the process and the outcome, and share this with someone you trust.

3. Visualize yourself succeeding in reaching the goals you have set for yourself. Do this consistently as part of your daily routine.

4. Once you know what success looks like, act as if it is already your reality. Dress, speak, and behave in ways that are consistent with your vision.

5. Establish boundaries with those around you who zap your energy, ask too much of you, or don't seem to respect your no. (Refer to "The Courage to Give and Receive Feedback" for more strategies related to having conversations.)

6. Stop asking for permission; instead find out what your boss and others expect from you, and agree with them up front about your span of control and authority.

7. Look out for others, but not at the cost of your own needs. Putting others' needs ahead of yours consistently is self-sabotaging. You count, too.

Notes

1. Nepo, Mark. *The Book of Awakening: Having the Life You Want by Being Present to the Life You Have*. San Francisco: Conari Press, 2000. Used with permission.

2. Covey, Stephen M. R. *The Speed of Trust: The One Thing That Changes Everything*. New York: Free Press, 2006.

3. Niles, Frank. "How to Use Visualization to Achieve Your Goals." *Huffington Post*, last revised August 17, 2011. http://www.huffingtonpost.com/frank-niles-phd/visualization-goals_b_878424.html.

4. Grant, Adam. *Give and Take: A Revolutionary Approach to Success*. New York: Viking, 2013.

6 The Courage to Delegate

Few things can help an individual more than to place responsibility on him, and to let him know that you trust him.[1]

—Booker T. Washington (emphasis added)

Mateo is a leader ready to move to the next level in his career. He had been very successful where he was for quite a long time. He knew how he was viewed in his division but not across his global organization. He wanted to know what others with whom he had interacted throughout the years outside of his immediate division thought of him. Mateo gave me a list of key leaders he wanted to work for in other parts of the company so that I could find out how they viewed his leadership potential.

To start the process, I crafted several questions to understand better how they perceived leadership and how they perceived Mateo. The questions I used were as follows:

1. What does it take to be a successful leader on your team/in your organization?

2. From your experience or from what you've observed, what do you believe are the leadership strengths Mateo would likely bring to your team/organization?

3. From your experience or from what you've observed, what do you believe are the areas in which Mateo would struggle or needs further development if he moved to your team/organization?

4. What additional insight or information do you have that would help Mateo continue to grow as a leader?

5. On a scale of 1 to 5, with 1 being "no way" and 5 being "without question," would you hire Mateo to lead in your organization?

Overwhelmingly, the leaders I spoke with agreed that Mateo was a superstar. They knew he was capable of much more than what he was doing, and they all agreed it was time for him to make a major career move. In terms of specific feedback, Mateo was most interested in knowing what one key leader (we'll call him Peter) had said when asked, "Would you hire Mateo to lead in your organization?" Peter was a leader Mateo worked with often and respected more than anyone else. Peter agreed with the others that he would hire Mateo but not for a more senior role. He said he would likely transfer Mateo to his department in a lateral position, rather than a promotion. When I asked him to explain this more, he said that he wasn't sure Mateo delegated and developed his people to the level that he would want a more senior leader in his organization to do. In fact, I knew from interviewing Mateo's team that this was true.

When asked to rate how well Mateo clearly and comfortably delegates both routine and important tasks and decisions, his team rated him a 3 when all other competencies rated were at 4 and 5 consistently. When I asked Peter to tell me how he knew that Mateo struggled with delegating and developing his people, he told me that whenever there was a problem and he needed Mateo's team to solve it, he would hear directly from Mateo and only Mateo. Peter felt that if Mateo were leveraging his team more effectively, he would be including them in high-stakes problem solving and giving them outside exposure. Peter acknowledged that Mateo might be doing a better job of delegating to his team when working with other groups, but he wasn't doing so with his.

When I shared this information with Mateo, he was disappointed but he didn't disagree. He said he knew he struggled with delegating to others. He said he felt like he could do it better than anyone else on his team. He feared that giving responsibility to others who could fail put his reputation at high risk, so he didn't delegate. Unfortunately, Mateo's choice not to delegate became the reason he would not be considered for a promotion by one of his most respected leaders.

At Personify Leadership, we define *delegation* as "sharing authority and responsibility with a delegate." We define the *delegate* as "someone who is authorized to represent the leader." For most leaders, these definitions cause an instant jab of pain right to the gut. Giving others power, giving others control, and giving others a chance to do what we do so well is risky. Very risky. Who in his right mind wants to take a risk when he can quickly maintain status quo by doing the job himself and ensure his reputation stays intact? Delegating to others requires a word we haven't explored much yet: *vulnerability*.

Dr. Brené Brown is a research professor at the University of Houston Graduate College of Social Work and best-selling author. She has spent the past twelve years studying vulnerability, courage, and worthiness. During an interview with Dan Schawbel in *Forbes*, Brown described the power of vulnerability this way: "When you shut down vulnerability, you shut down opportunity."[2]

These words could not be truer than when you apply them to delegation. Mateo lacked the willingness to fail or have others fail. In other words, he lacked the willingness to be vulnerable. The consequence of not being vulnerable was that he was unable to exercise an opportunity for growth and advancement. From my experience in working with leaders all over the world, this is true in general. It's a small minority who learn to overcome what we at Personify Leadership refer to as the Delegation Doom Loop (Figure 6.1).

The Delegation Doom Loop looks something like this: I don't delegate because the (potential) delegate is unskilled. Why is the

Figure 6.1 Delegation Doom Loop

delegate unskilled? Because I don't delegate. I continue not delegating to this person, and therefore, the team member remains unskilled. And round and round it goes. As a result, we continue to do the work ourselves, and the other individual never develops new skills. Here are some of the most common responses to why leaders don't delegate:

- Delegation takes too much time.
- I feel guilty giving my team more work.
- I like being the superstar.
- I am afraid my people won't do it as well as I would.
- My customer wants only me.
- I don't have the people to delegate to.

A survey of 332 companies found that 46 percent of companies have a "somewhat high" or "high" level of concern about their workers' delegation skills,[3] which means that just slightly less than half of leaders commonly fall into the Delegation Doom Loop. Most of us don't need a research study to tell us this; it's a familiar experience. But the question on everyone's mind is "Why?" If we know we are perpetuating a cycle that will not produce good results, why do we continue to do it? The answer goes back to our fundamental understanding of courage. We believe the pain associated with delegating is worse than the pain of doing the work ourselves. If you recall from "The Courage to Get Unstuck," the pain of change is part of the pain of delegation. We don't want to traverse our way through the cold and hungry part of change to get to a more sustainable and productive place of warm and full, so we stay in warm and hungry. It isn't until we are overlooked for promotions or find ourselves unable to scale our business to the size the market demands that we begin to realize warm and hungry is no longer an option. It's hard; I get it. But is the alternative—stuck in the Doom Loop with limited opportunities—worth it to you? Do you want to end up a delegation statistic, or do you want to do something different?

Leveraging the other facets of courage we've discussed so far, consider what you already know to help you get there.

- Consider "The Courage to Take a Stand"—what does it say about what we value if we do all the work and save the best, most visible projects for ourselves?

- Consider "The Courage to Get Unstuck"—similar to Mateo, do we want to be somewhere else? Are we holding ourselves or others back?

- Consider "The Courage to Be Humble"—what does it say about us if our egos can't let go of responsibility and authority? What does it say about us if we think we're the only ones who can do it right?

- Consider "The Courage to Be Confident"—what does it say about our confidence in others if we don't trust them to fail temporarily so that they can grow long term? What does it say about our own self-confidence if we don't trust ourselves to fail temporarily so that we can grow long term? Let's end the Delegation Doom Loop by making a declaration to be and do something different:

  I am a leader who delegates authority and responsibility (value) so that others and I can grow (get unstuck) and contribute amazing things to my team and organization (humility and confidence).

Now, let's look at the obstacles to delegation one by one and discuss how to look at them differently so that we can live this declaration in our daily life.

Delegation Takes Too Much Time

I'll start by asking this question "How much time have you spent in the Doom Loop?" Chances are months, maybe even years. Nothing can be more of a waste of time than repeating the same behaviors over and over expecting a change. That's the definition of insanity.

Brooke was recently promoted to project director, which meant she was no longer responsible for managing the day-to-day of the projects with her team but instead overseeing the entire project team with no involvement in project management. She had a team of five. However, two of her team positions were open with no qualified candidates to fill them, one employee on a leave of absence, and another on a performance improvement plan, leaving only three employees who were really capable of carrying the workload. We agreed the most important thing she could do would be to hire two qualified team members and manage the performance of the lower performer. Unfortunately, Brooke could not pull herself out of her daily tasks long enough to do either. I asked her why she wasn't delegating more to her team so that she could focus her energy on her priorities. She said it was just faster if she did it herself. A year went by and Brooke hired another individual, but unfortunately, it was not a good hire and that employee left within two months. The employee on leave came back, but the employee on the performance improvement plan was let go from the organization. All in all, she was in just about the same position as a year before.

What's even more unfortunate for Brooke was that, as a result of not delegating, she didn't do that great a job at the project director level, and she was eventually demoted.

The magic question is "How do I create time for myself to delegate when the thing that will create time is delegation?" Regrettably, I don't have a magic answer. But I do have some suggestions:

1. Assess what is on your plate that can be postponed or dropped. Not everything we do is necessary. Some of what we do is because we've always done it, the person before us in the role always did it, and the person before them, and so on.

2. Look at ways to streamline your day so that you are always focusing your energy on your top two or three priorities.

3. Change expectations of outcomes. If you don't have the right team in place with the right skill level to manage a traditional workload, maybe it's time to change the workload temporarily. We don't always have control over this, but we can influence others who do. The goal here is to buy you time to use delegation as a developmental process.

4. Manage your energy in other parts of your life so that you can temporarily do more of the strategic stuff at work that gets you unstuck (like hiring a qualified team).

5. As requests for your time come in, practice asking, "*Why* this task and *why* me and my team?" rather than "*When* do you want it done?"

The most important thing to know about creating time for yourself and your team is that you have more control to do this than you think. If you read this list of suggestions and mentally said, "That will never work," then you've already lost the battle. You can do much to influence the way work gets done for you and your team.

I Feel Guilty Giving My Team More Work

It's not uncommon to feel guilty delegating more work to someone who already has a lot on his or her plate. However, when we don't delegate, we aren't doing our part as leaders to provide opportunities for others to develop. Instead of thinking about how you are increasing someone's workload, think about how you are using delegation to help him or her grow. In this way, we can reframe our guilt—or shift our thinking about delegation. To delegate well as a developmental process means being thoughtful about the assignments, projects, or tasks we hand over to our team members. It's not something we do in haste. Ask your team member what it is he or she is doing that he or she can give to someone else (or stop doing) that frees up time and what is it he or she wants to do that you're doing. See where the conversation goes from there.

It's also important to remember as you are delegating that you count too. If you are not delegating what you need to because others are not prepared to handle it, you're not making your needs equally as important as others' needs. It's true that leaders rarely get to put their needs above their team's. But they need to manage their energy boundaries, or they'll be of no use to their organization or their team as a long-term, sustainable resource. Leaders also need to be able to scale their role so that they can scale the organization. It's nearly impossible to be strategic when you're stuck in the weeds.

Finally, consider that part of your role as a leader is to allow others to struggle to some extent before stepping in to lighten their load, however counterintuitive that might seem. Teaching my kids to read has been a very challenging endeavor for me for exactly this reason. My natural inclination is to step in and solve the problem. My very tenacious daughter, whose first phrase was "all by myself," said to me at bedtime one night, "Ugh, Mom, stop trying to help me. I'm reading the book, not you!" That was the goal, but I kept butting in with my insatiable need to move things along. Coaching employees isn't far off. When we step in before they struggle a little, we rob them of the opportunity to learn for themselves. Let them see how far they can go.

In the best-selling book *Living with a SEAL*, author Jesse Itzler writes about David Goggins and the Navy SEALs' 40 Percent Rule, which basically states: "When you think you are finished, you still have 40 percent left." Think about marathoners, for example. Most marathoners complete the race even when they feel like they've hit the wall. That's because when the racer feels the pain of being depleted, it's an indication he or she has 40 percent in reserves left to go. Likewise, letting our people carry their workload and more gives them an opportunity to see how far they can go. It allows them to tap into their reserves and challenge themselves to achieve more.[4]

I Love Doing It All—or at Least Being the Superstar

Andy is a superstar. Just ask any of his clients. At a moment's notice, he will jump on a plane and land where the nearest crisis exists and put out the fire. He thrives on the adrenaline of swooping in and saving the day. He admitted to me that it would be hard for him to give up that part of his job—ever. On the other hand, Andy is struggling with delegation. It's hard for his team to get the direction and development they need from him when he is traveling all over the continent solving problems. During our discussions, he said he believes he is actually a better leader because he is willing to do the hard work. I told him that may not necessarily be true. To offer a different perspective, I shared with him Mateo's story and how being the superstar limited his potential for being considered for a promotion. This made Andy stop and think.

Like Andy, there are ways to still be a superstar *and* delegate and develop others well. It starts with reframing how you see your role as a superstar. If you believe superstar is only about doing the work, eventually you'll have to decide whether you want to be a fantastic, over-the-top individual contributor or you want to be a leader. If your choice is leadership, consider a superstar leader as being an exceptional developer of people.

I learned this lesson the hard way, and I would say it represents one of my most humbling experiences. At one point in my career,

I went from a department of one to a department of four. I had been the superstar individual contributor for a couple of years, but as the team expanded, other talent emerged. I had one exceptional team member we'll call Tracey. Tracey had great potential. Even though I wanted her to succeed, I wasn't ready to share the spotlight with her. I was relishing it myself. It didn't occur to me that it was much of an issue until the CEO, a man I respected and trusted, shared some tough feedback. I had just finished presenting and leading a formal executive leadership event where Tracey sat watching. He said to me, "Angela, Tracey will never shine in your shadow." He didn't provide any specifics. I guess he figured his feedback was obvious enough to understand, and if I didn't get it, there was a much larger problem at hand. But I did get it. His words humbled me. I realized I had hoarded opportunities for myself and limited hers. It was a lesson I'll never forget.

Superstar individual contributors are naturally blind to the need for them to shift to becoming exceptional developers of people. Everything the superstar has learned so far in his or her career rewards *his or her* superior performance, not others'. When they are promoted to leadership positions, most superstars, unfortunately, never get the appropriate support to help them make the transition. This leads them to rely on the tools they already have—not the ones they have yet to develop. Learning to be an exceptional developer of people is a transition and does not happen overnight. If you find yourself here, find a superstar developer of people to learn from. If you've been the superstar individual contributor turned developer of people, offer your guidance to those who can learn from you.

Don't underestimate the beauty in this transition. Giving others the spotlight can be incredibly rewarding. No matter where your people go, even if they shine so brightly that they are promoted outside your team or outside the organization, they will always be a reflection of you.

I Am Afraid My People Won't Do It as Well as I Would

How many of you have said to yourself or out loud to others, "I don't delegate because I'm afraid my people won't do it as well as I would"? Okay, I have some validating words to share. *You are right.* They won't do it better than you, at least not at first. But they may be able to do it better in the long run. Or they may do it differently and unexpectedly add innovation and creativity to your team.

Part of what makes it tough to let others struggle, get it wrong, learn from it, and finally do it as well as, if not better than, you is that most organizations don't embrace failure as a learning tool. Creating tolerance for failure is a number one priority for the leader who needs to delegate. Of course, when you begin talking about creating a tolerance for failure, you start hearing whispers about simultaneously creating a culture without accountability. But the two can be mutually exclusive. If you want to remove fear of failure but maintain accountability, consider how you are managing failure in your organization today. Does every failure have the same consequence? Does the intention of the team member factor into your decision? What about the *reason* for failure?

Amy Edmondson, a professor at Harvard, believes widely held beliefs about failure in the workplace are misguided. Failure can be bad, it can be inevitable, and it can be good. In a *Harvard Business Review* article titled "Strategies for Learning from Failure," she describes preventable failures in a predictable operation as different from unavoidable failures in a complex system and intelligent failures on the frontier as different from both the preventable and the unavoidable.[5]

What exactly is an intelligent failure? Duke University professor of management Sim Sitkin coined the phrase "intelligent failure" as a way to describe a process for proactively creating an environment in which people can experiment, be creative, practice, and learn from failures. If we consider developing our people as an intelligent step toward expanding the frontier of our team's capacity and, as a result, our organization's capacity, then intelligent failure is the way to go.[6]

To better understand intelligent failure, let's look at some examples. While attending my kid's school play, I found myself sitting next to an irritated dad. He was distracted, and visibly upset, checking his phone every few seconds. I asked him what was going on, and he shared with me frustrations he had with his sales manager. A multimillion-dollar deal was on the table, and without any preparation on the proposal, his sales manager had decided to meet with the client. Things did not go well. The salesperson did not understand some of the nuances of the proposal and did not have an adequate understanding of the history of the relationship to the client. Needless to say, there was cause for concern. This was the kind of failure that could have been prevented.

On the other hand, Colin Powell shares a story of a team's intelligent failure in his book *It Worked for Me: In Life and Leadership*.[7] Instead of providing a security briefing to the president directly, he chose to delegate it to his team. The team was very excited about the opportunity and did everything they could to prepare. Powell also informed the president that the briefing would be led by his team to ensure the president supported this attempt at delegation, even if there was some level of failure. As it turns out, the team did an excellent job, impressing the president and Powell. However, Powell explains that, had the briefing gone poorly, he knew this would have been informative for him. If his team had not been able to brief the president adequately, he would've gained valuable insight into their capabilities. This is an example of intelligent failure, failure that brings about needed information to grow and develop people and the organization.

Personify Leadership's entire first year in the market was one failure after another, some intelligent, some not. There were some successes sprinkled in there as well. We've lived to tell the tale. My business partner and I had designed the Personify Leadership program after first being experts in our individual fields, and second, being business entrepreneurs. To let go and give others authority and responsibility of our baby (not to mention our life savings) was a radical shift for both of us. As the principals behind the work, it made the most sense that together, we would keep delivering our program to our customers and leading our certification courses for other facilitators. Until one day it just didn't make sense anymore. Our calendars were so busy working *in* the organization that we couldn't work *on* the organization. After relatively static growth between year one and year two, we decided we would have to delegate to take our organization to the next level. We trained other facilitators to work with us and, eventually, in place of us. The result was evident by year three, when we grew by 125 percent. Looking back, it was the smartest thing we ever did for our organization.

My Customer Wants Only Me

Rachel was promoted with increasing responsibility because of her stellar reputation and work ethic. In addition, Rachel inherited a very capable and motivated team, who accepted responsibility and authority. However, even though Rachel wanted to delegate and step into her new role, her customer was reluctant. He liked working with Rachel and Rachel only.

Rachel decided the way to change this without alienating the client would be to get the client involved in the delegation process. She began by briefing the customer on her developmental goals in her new position as well as her new responsibilities. She shared how important it was to her to succeed in this new role and at the same time make a successful transition for her client and her team. She explained the benefits of the transition to the client. With Rachel working at a more strategic level, she would have the opportunity to help the client take a longer-term view of their partnership while bringing someone with new and creative ideas to work in her place. The client expressed concerns about the learning curve, and together they agreed on how they would work with the new team member to shorten the curve. Rachel made the client a partner in the delegation process to ensure a win-win for everyone.

Samuel had a different challenge. Every time he introduced himself to a new client as the face of his team, the client was reluctant to work with anyone else. Samuel realized he had to find ways to remove himself from the front-end client relationship-building phase and allow his clients to connect with other team members *before* he stepped in. Otherwise, he would forever be doing the work once the contract was signed. He also learned that if he did choose to be a part of the front-end client relationship-building phase, he would have to be firm about when his role ended and where other team members' roles began. Like Andy and me, Samuel liked being the superstar, so before he could change the dynamic with the customer, he had to change how he viewed his role as the leader.

I Don't Have People to Delegate to

Maybe you're reading this chapter thinking to yourself, *None of this applies to me because I don't have direct reports. I'm a department of one.* Or maybe you're a project manager responsible for getting projects done without a team. If so, you're not alone. This is what we call in Personify Leadership the new delegation paradigm. If we describe a paradigm as "a way of thinking, or a way of viewing something," we can define a paradigm shift as "a fundamental change in your viewpoint, or your perspective." Our fundamental thinking about delegation has been the traditional top-down model. If you report to me, I'm authorized to give you work and you're required to do it. However, this model has not evolved much as organizations have shifted how they operate. Rarely do we just have a direct-line manager up top; we usually have a dotted-line leader as well. In addition, we have responsibilities to create and lead change throughout the organization with no direct reports and no direct authority. This changes how we approach delegation and how we think about delegation. This requires a new delegation paradigm that represents a matrix organization.

In this new paradigm, getting work done through others who don't report to us may seem more difficult, but in reality, it's not much different from the top-down model. We are fooling ourselves as leaders if we believe we have complete authority over people just because they report to us. Our people still have the ability to veto us; they just don't always say it aloud. Instead, the veto comes in the form of subtle and sometimes outright sabotage. The sabotage can show up as resistance, negative watercooler talk, missed work, and low performance and effort. The solution to sabotage is to treat your delegates as individuals with voice and choice, able to share their thoughts and feedback and say no if they don't agree with your delegated request. Working without direct reports requires building relationships with your potential delegates, allowing them to share their voices, and giving them choices. In this way, the skills a leader learns delegating to nondirect reports prepares them to be exceptional delegators when they have their own direct-report teams.

Delegating in the new paradigm also means a leader needs to manage up, across, and down in the organization. The first step is partnering up front with peers, the boss, and the boss's peers about the work initiatives they represent and how they will work together to meet one another's expectations. The role of delegation in the new paradigm is as much about interpersonal savvy and political savvy as it is about developing others. Let's look at an example of a leader who does this well.

Sasha is a vice president of talent development for a privately held transportation company in the North Pacific. Like many companies suffering from the flood of baby boomers retiring, her company is losing top talent rapidly. To adjust the trajectory of this path, Sasha was hired to create an enterprise-wide talent development strategy. The strategy includes sharing talent across six organizations that operate completely independently of one another. As part of this process, Sasha has lofty goals, a decent budget, and limited head count. What she needs to accomplish enterprise wide will happen only if she leverages the human resources directors and their teams at each company.

To get buy-in and support up front, Sasha invited all the company HR members to the enterprise headquarters for a team meeting. She began the meeting by giving each team the opportunity to share what their group does, what they are proud of, and what they feel are their challenges. During the meeting, they learned a lot about one another and gained an appreciation for one another's expertise and goals. Sasha also shared the enterprise vision, which included leveraging each of them and their teams. She also invited the enterprise CEO to speak at the meeting, reinforcing Sasha's vision for the team. Sasha then invited her delegates to define their own level of commitment to the enterprise strategy and the timeline in which they would be able to execute their commitments. By the time the meetings wrapped up and everyone was on the way back home, Sasha had successfully created a team of delegates who did not work directly for her but were ready to do the work needed to make things happen. Over time, there have inevitably been struggles and setbacks, but the focus and commitment have not wavered.

Breaking out of the Delegation Doom Loop requires time management, being willing to let your team struggle a little, stepping out of the spotlight, creating a culture of intelligent failure, involving the customer in the delegation process, and navigating a new paradigm. It takes courage, but it is possible. You just have to be willing to stick it out past warm and hungry to warm and full.

Chapter Application

Questions to Consider

1. How well do you actually meet the application of this courage statement? *I am a leader who delegates authority and responsibility (value) so that others and I can grow (get unstuck) and contribute amazing things to my team and organization (humility and confidence).*

2. Are there things you need to do to improve your ability to reflect the above statement? If so, what specifically are you committed to doing differently?

3. Do you struggle with the Delegation Doom Loop? If so, how will you break out of the cycle?

Strategies for Delegating

1. Share authority and responsibility with another person whom you will authorize to represent you.

2. Identify strategies for managing your time provided in this chapter so that you free up more time to focus on delegation.

3. Challenge your people to tap into their reserves and see how much more they can achieve.

4. Share the spotlight. Your people are always a reflection of you, so when they shine, you shine.

5. Your people won't do it as well as you if you don't develop them. Start by selecting someone you feel has demonstrated the ability to leverage learning opportunities, and invest your time in his or her growth.

6. Delegation is not just a tool for people who have direct reports. It's for anyone who has work he or she needs to get done through others. Identify people who can support you (inside or outside of the organization) to get work done.

Notes

1. Booker T. Washington Society. "Quotations by Booker T. Washington: Time-less, Common Sense Wisdom." Accessed December 2, 2016. http://www.btwsociety.org/library/misc/quotes.php.

2. Schawbel, Dan. "Brené Brown: How Vulnerability Can Make Our Lives Better," *Forbes*, April 21, 2013. http://www.forbes.com/sites/danschawbel/2013/04/21/brene-brown-how-vulnerability-can-make-our-lives-better/#57b3a40160ba.

3. i4cp. "You Want It When?" June 26, 2007. http://www.i4cp.com/news/2007/06/26/you-want-it-when.

4. Itzler, Jesse. *Living with a SEAL: 31 Days Training with the Toughest Man on the Planet.* New York: Center Street, 2015.

5. Edmondson, Amy C. "Strategies for Learning from Failure." *Harvard Business Review*, April 2011. https://hbr.org/2011/04/strategies-for-learning-from-failure.

6. Helliwell, Laura. "Innovation Through 'Intelligent Failure.'" Harvard Business Publishing Corporate Learning. September 29, 2014. http://www.harvardbusiness.org/blog/innovation-through-%E2%80%9Cintelligent-failure%E2%80%9D.

7. Powell, Colin. *It Worked for Me: In Life and Leadership.* With Tony Koltz. New York: HarperCollins, 2012.

7 The Courage to Give and Receive Feedback

There's no coming to consciousness without pain.[1]

—Carl G. Jung

Shane is a leader known for turning poor performers into productive team members. After taking on a new role, he was given Beth. Beth is the kind of employee who toggles between meeting expectations and underperforming. Every time Shane thinks she is starting to turn a corner, he will get feedback from a peer or a customer that Beth has disappointed him or her again. Shane has isolated Beth from large tasks assigned to her role and has changed the scope and environment in which she operates so that he can mitigate her ineffectiveness and continue development efforts. But all of this has fallen short of any tangible results. Once highly effective at developing team members, Shane has begun to question his own abilities as a leader.

I asked Shane to tell me about how Beth came to his team. He shared with me that his boss, Craig, had asked him to take Beth on and attempt to rehabilitate her performance. Apparently, Craig had failed to get results with Beth and was hoping Shane would have a different outcome. Later, in a conversation with Craig, I asked him how Beth came to join his team. Craig said that *his* boss, the chief financial officer, had requested that he take Beth to his team because she had been struggling where she was. I decided to talk with Beth to better understand how it came to be that she was moved to three teams in four years.

According to Beth, she was not provided much clarity about why she was being transferred from one group to another. She described feeling bounced around like a beach ball, not sure where she'd end up next. She said over the years she had been provided different explanations for the changes. The first time she was told that her strengths would be better leveraged in a role that was not customer facing. When she was moved again, she was told she would be more successful assisting another team. The last time, when she was transitioned onto Shane's team, she was told she had a skill set that Shane's team required. It's clear the feedback Beth received did not mirror the experiences others were actually having with her. Beth was being buffered from some of the most valid and useful information available. Each time she was moved along, she was given a diluted message or one that largely avoided facts. Instead of providing Beth with tough and necessary feedback about her lack of performance, she was passed along from one team to another in the hope that someone else would have the courage to deal with the situation more effectively.

How often does this situation happen in the workplace? Too often to count. As a matter of fact, the only thing more common than a leader not giving feedback is the leader's lack of interest in receiving feedback—or at least in the way he or she is used to receiving it. Most leaders prefer getting useful feedback; however, most leaders don't actually give useful feedback, but rather, a diluted version of it. So why is it leaders want feedback but don't like receiving it and leaders responsible for giving feedback don't give it well? The answer is because both giving and receiving useful feedback require courage. Let me be clear; there is feedback that is great to give and receive and doesn't necessarily require courage, but that's not the kind of feedback I'm talking about. I'm talking about the big, hairy, audacious feedback that makes you squirm just thinking about it. That's the kind of feedback we'll tackle in this chapter.

The Big Temptation and Courageous Feedback

When it comes to giving feedback, there is the feedback conversation we have in our head, the feedback conversation we actually have, and the feedback conversation we need to have. Going back to our opening story of Shane and Beth, the feedback conversation in our head about how to address Beth's performance usually goes something like "Beth, I don't have time to deal with this. Please get your act together." But most of us have enough composure not to say this. So instead what we say is, "Beth, mostly you're doing well. Just step it up a bit." Which demonstrates effort but is not useful.

How about this: *Beth, I care about your success, so it's important to me that we talk about some of the things happening right now around your performance. In the past you've struggled with consistently meeting expectations. You'll hit a deadline or meet a commitment once, maybe even twice, then fall back into a pattern of missing deadlines and commitments. As a result, I can't be sure I can count on you to come through on the next commitment. Others who are interdependent on you to deliver on their commitments feel similarly and continue to share their disappointment with me. This is a pattern that has to stop. Can you help me understand how you see it?*

The Big Temptation that Father Bob spoke of in "The Business Case for Courage" is not only the temptation to avoid action but also the temptation to avoid giving and receiving feedback. It pains us to our core to say something to others that is difficult for us to say or for them to hear. Therefore, the Big Temptation with feedback is to say what is easier to say and what is easier for the other person to hear. If we fall into the Big Temptation and avoid giving and receiving feedback, we go into the cycle of avoid, create, and avoid or avoid, suppress, and avoid.

I'll never forget facilitating a class with a group of leaders on the topic of difficult feedback. About halfway through the class I noticed the group starting to squirm a little, looking uncomfortable and a bit unsure what to do with themselves. I looked around the room to see what might be happening to create this discomfort but nothing seemed apparent. Although I continued to facilitate, it started to feel almost pointless. I was losing the group's interest, and I was completely unsure as to what I was doing wrong. I was sensing frustration from them and I was definitely frustrated. Finally, one woman had the courage to stand up, lead me out into the middle of the hallway, and point out that the third button down on my white, tailored shirt was undone, and my shirt was gaping wide open. I was mortified! I quickly put myself back together and reunited with my class, who were all completely relieved that finally the cat was out of the bag. I was no longer working against my own interest trying desperately to connect with a group that was trying desperately to overlook me.

Think about how much energy we waste by skirting around the real issue. Often, when we choose to withhold feedback, we think we are being nice or diplomatic, but in reality, we're just being flat-out scaredy pants. The true irony of this story is withholding feedback from people who would otherwise benefit from it is not nice. Far from it! Feedback is what allows us to see what is otherwise invisible to us. It is a powerful flashlight that allows us to work in the light rather than the dark. Giving feedback is a respectful and caring way to say *I believe in you and I want you to succeed*. Without it we give others a false sense of security in their less-than-desirable performance.

Being courageous enough to provide useful feedback means saying what needs to be said, rather than what is easier to say, and saying what needs to be said, rather than what is easier for the other person to hear. In our personal lives and at work, we need to give and receive feedback before, during, and after tough times. We give feedback *before* tough times so that we can prevent the tough time from happening or mitigate the extent to which we experience it. *During* tough times, giving and receiving feedback helps us be clearer and move through our challenges more quickly. *After* tough times, we need feedback to help us learn from the experience. If you recall from the chapter "The Courage to Get Unstuck," I shared the formula Pain + Meaning = Growth. When we give and receive feedback before, during, or after tough times, we are adding meaning to the situation around us, helping ourselves and others transform our pain into a growth experience.

The Feedback Trifecta—Giving Feedback

The most difficult feedback to give is usually the most necessary to hear, and yet it largely goes undelivered. This is because of what I call the feedback trifecta. Leaders responsible for delivering the feedback lack the *courage* to do it, the *skills* needed to give feedback are under-developed, and the typical workplace *environment* unknowingly and sometimes knowingly promotes avoiding honest and open communication. And organizations pay for it.

Natalia, a neighbor and dear friend of mine who is a dentist in south Florida, called me this morning with a story she said she had to share. She said, "Angela, I know this is applicable to other business leaders so I wanted to share it with you so that you could share it with them." Natalia is a busy woman, an entrepreneur, a mom, and a wife, so it goes without saying her time is limited. She is also an incredibly kind and loving person. If you've met Natalia, you feel you know her. She is nice, but a doormat she is not, as you will quickly learn.

Natalia's story starts when she received a text from her nail technician that she had to cancel her appointment for her manicure 30 minutes before her appointment time. (To the men reading this story, the answer is yes, I'm going to talk about manicures here for a minute, but stick with me. I promise there is a bigger purpose to this story that's relevant to your gender as well!). She said the technician explained in her text that she had a difficult client arrive without an appointment. She said it was too hard to say no to the difficult client, and because Natalia was so nice and accommodating she knew she would understand. Natalia did accommodate her and instead booked her appointment for the following day. When she arrived for her appointment the next day, her nail technician had another client with her. Natalia waited for 30 minutes but then had to leave. When she confronted the technician about the situation on her way out the door, the technician said that once again she was in a tough spot with a difficult client and decided to take the client in place of Natalia. But this time, Natalia wasn't so eager to accommodate her. Natalia explained, in a nice way of course, that even though she was understanding by nature, the situation wasn't acceptable, and she would be leaving that day and taking her business with her.

It goes without saying that Natalia was frustrated. She thought about how the experience related to her work as a business leader. There were many times in which she pushed back a date or time for a good or understanding client to accommodate a difficult client who was arguing and complaining. It took her experiencing this behavior herself *as the client* to see how her personal leadership choices were affecting her own client base.

She went back to her office and told her staff, "Don't ever feel like our good clients are going to be here forever. If we accommodate our bad clients instead of sharing our concerns and put off our good clients, in the end we'll be stuck with a business full of bad clients."

Courage

Natalia's example is one of countless examples of where we don't say what needs to be said because we fear the pain that comes with giving feedback. Bottom line, there will be pain when giving feedback because saying what needs to be said has consequences. Remember the feel, think, feel model that leads to reaction or action I shared in "The Business Case for Courage"? We know that if we say what is not easy to say or easy for the other person to hear, we are going to engage the other person in this process. What we don't know is whether it will end with *reaction* or *action*. Those receiving our feedback will likely ask themselves questions about our motive. If they choose to assume bad motive and choose an emotion of fear, they will likely choose a reaction of shutting down and shutting us out. It's possible they could choose to lash out with words intended to hurt us back. The tough consequence of giving feedback is that we can't choose for others how they choose to hear our words. More important, we can't choose for others what they choose to do with them. We don't like that feedback leads to people we care about and work with avoiding us, holding grudges against us, and lashing out at us. We don't like being the villain when they choose to be the victim. This is why giving feedback takes courage. The choice we have is to shy away from it, provide it haphazardly, or give it skillfully and courageously.

Skill

A mounting body of evidence from researchers and practitioners tells us positive words and interactions with others are at the heart of engagement and strong performance.[2–4] And yet, sometimes giving feedback is a positive experience and sometimes it is not. Hearing the tough stuff usually doesn't make us feel very engaged or leave us wanting to perform. Our goal, then, is to find a way to say the hard stuff while engaging others. The opportunity lies in understanding the power of our words. Whether we are aware of it or not, our words either encourage or discourage others. The word *encourage* means "to inspire courage in others." The word *discourage* means "to cause someone to lose courage."

Take a moment and imagine someone whom you respect and look up to, someone who is important to you. Imagine sitting in front of this person, and he or she says these words:

"You are incompetent."

"I don't trust you."

"I've lost respect for you."

What emotions do you feel now? How do you feel about yourself? What are you motivated to do because of these emotions? For most of us, when we hear this kind of feedback from someone important to us, we feel angry, sad, misunderstood, and betrayed. Our natural response is to fight back, flee from the situation, or freeze in place. But the last thing we want is to believe it's true or do something about it. I remember the last time I got feedback from a friend that wasn't pleasant to hear. I felt deeply betrayed and angry. The more I thought about it, the angrier I got. I wanted to justify my behaviors, I wanted a new friend, and I wanted to rewind and pretend I never heard the feedback. The last thing I was ready to do at the time was actually accept the feedback and do something about it. Now, imagine someone important to you says these words:

"I believe in you."

"You've got this."

"You are amazing."

What emotions do you feel now? How do you feel about yourself? What are you motivated to do because of these emotions? Contrary to my friend who gave me harsh feedback, I had a boss who was very good at giving positive feedback. He told me how important I was, he shared how confident he was in my abilities, and he communicated his trust in my decision-making ability. This is a boss I would have followed off a cliff.

Here is the thing about feedback. It is personal. Even when we don't intend for our words to be personal, they are. Feedback is our way of describing how the other person shows up in our world. Even when we use factual data in our feedback, we strike the emotional chords of the other person. Our words have emotional weight.

When we give feedback, no matter what our message is, our goal should be to encourage—inspire courage—in others. Therefore, the skill necessary to inspire courage is: *Say what needs to be said in a way that others will hear it, with respect and concern for the other person, while staying true to the virtue of the message.*

Some specific things we can do to increase our skill in giving feedback include minimizing the threat we represent, showing empathy, using exploratory language rather than absolutes, and demonstrating compassionate persistence.

Minimize the Threat We Represent   Giving feedback that inspires courage and moves others to action (not reaction) requires minimizing the threat we represent. As the feedback giver, we are not outside the process but within the process. And when you're inside the process of receiving feedback, you are vulnerable. This means that the feedback giver should mirror the receiver's vulnerability. One way to do this is start the feedback process by sharing the intention behind what you are sharing and setting a nonthreatening but supportive tone for the conversation (see Table 7.1).

Table 7.1 Minimize the Threat We Represent

Threatening	Nonthreatening
Sarah, I have your results here, and they are not good. What is the problem? I thought when I hired you, you were capable of more.	*Sarah, I want to see you succeed. I know that you are capable of more than you are achieving right now, which is why it's important to me to share with you what I'm seeing that might help you.*
Outcome: loss of courage and moves the person to reaction	Outcome: inspires courage and moves the person to action

Show Empathy   True empathy is to literally feel what someone else is feeling. The role of empathy in feedback is to acknowledge how the other person is feeling. When we do this, we allow the emotion to surface and find its appropriate place in the conversation. If we ignore the emotion or pretend it's not there, we become even more of a threat to the other person (see Table 7.2).

Table 7.2 Show Empathy

Feedback Without Empathy	Feedback with Empathy
Regardless of the workload, there are quality standards and deadlines, period. Complaints and excuses won't get the job done.	*I understand that you are struggling with a tough workload. I imagine there are days it feels overwhelming. I'd like to see that your performance stays strong regardless of the workload. I realize that won't be easy but let's discuss it. From your perspective, is there a way this is possible?*
Outcome: loss of courage and moves the person to reaction	Outcome: inspires courage and moves the person to action

Use Exploratory Language Versus Absolutes   When we are providing feedback, the language we use can be critical to the outcome. Using absolutes, such as *always, never, none, can't, all, just,* and *only,* may back our receiver into a corner and make him or her feel judged and defensive. Instead, try using exploratory language that owns the feedback and demonstrates a willingness to be open. Exploratory language includes phrases such as "I'm wondering if…" "Have you considered…" "I'd like to share some thoughts I have," and "Can I explore this with you further?" When we are using exploratory language, we are inviting the other person to consider our perspective as a perspective, not as an absolute. In doing so, we minimize the threat our words represent (see Table 7.3).

Table 7.3 Use Exploratory Language Versus Absolutes

Absolute Language	Exploratory Language
You are always behind schedule. I can never count on you to deliver on time.	*I'm wondering if what's getting in the way is a lack of follow-through from others on the team that slows down the assembly line by the time it gets to you. Is that part of the challenge?*
Outcome: loss of courage and moves the person to reaction	Outcome: inspires courage and moves the person to action

Demonstrate Compassionate Persistence   Compassionate persistence requires staying true to the message regardless of the pushback the giver might receive from the receiver of the feedback. It also means not allowing the message to be derailed, deflected, or diluted. This can be extremely tough sometimes when others don't want to hear feedback. We are tempted to change *our message* so that others can hear it rather than change *how we deliver it* so that others can hear it (see Table 7.4).

Table 7.4 Compassionate Persistence Example One

Message Derailed and Deflected	Compassionate Persistence
SAM: Brian, I'm struggling with trust in our working relationship. At times, you'll go around me and share problems with my leadership without sharing them with me first. When this happens, I wonder if you don't feel comfortable talking with me, or worse, I wonder if you are intending to cause problems. I know you're under a lot of pressure, and it's probably easier to go around me. I get it. But I'm really hoping we can work things out together.	*SAM: Brian, I'm struggling with trust in our working relationship. At times, you'll go around me and share problems with my leadership without sharing them with me first. When this happens, I wonder if you don't feel comfortable talking with me, or worse, I wonder if you are intending to cause problems. I know you're under a lot of pressure, and it's probably easier to go around me. I get it. But I'm really hoping we can work things out together.*

(continued)

Table 7.4 *(continued)*

Message Derailed and Deflected	Compassionate Persistence
BRIAN: *We don't have a problem, Sam. I trust you.*	BRIAN: *We don't have a problem, Sam. I trust you.*
SAM: *I'm glad you feel that way, Brian, but part of what I'm hoping to communicate is the developing lack of trust I am feeling.*	SAM: *I'm glad you feel that way, Brian, but part of what I'm hoping to communicate is the developing lack of trust I am feeling.*
BRIAN: *I don't know what the problem is. I said I trust you. I am confident there is not a problem.*	BRIAN: *I don't know what the problem is. I said I trust you. I am confident there is not a problem.*
SAM: *Okay, just thought I'd share my concerns.*	SAM: *I'm sorry, Brian, I'm not trying to beat a dead horse. I just don't think we're on the same page. What I mean to convey is that I don't always trust that you are going to inform or involve me appropriately before you go to my leadership. I'm hoping that as we talk about this, I can better understand why that is and get a commitment from you to talk with me first before escalating your concerns.*
	BRIAN: *Jeez, Sam, you won't let this go will you? Fine, if it's that important to you, I'll come to you first. I'm not trying to go around you, just get things done. You don't always move quick enough, and I don't want you to hold things up.*
	SAM: *Brian, thank you for that feedback. I didn't realize I was holding things up. Let's talk about that more.*

Compassionate persistence keeps the conversation centered on the issue at hand. The difference between being derailed and staying the course is not about rigidity but about maintaining focus. Here is another example of how a message that requires compassionate persistence can get derailed (see Table 7.5).

Table 7.5 Compassionate Persistence Example Two

Message Derailed and Deflected	Compassionate Persistence
BRITNEY: Charles, I have something important I need to talk with you about.	BRITNEY: Charles, I have something important I need to talk with you about.
CHARLES: Okay.	CHARLES: Okay.
BRITNEY: I haven't gotten over last week's event. I know you feel differently but I feel like you gave up too quickly on the course of action we had agreed to. At times when things get stressful, you can make knee-jerk decisions that are not always good decisions.	BRITNEY: I haven't gotten over last week's event. I know you feel differently but I feel like you gave up too quickly on the course of action we had agreed to. At times when things get stressful, you can make knee-jerk decisions that are not always good decisions.
CHARLES: I don't make bad decisions. I can't believe after all the years we've worked together you still don't trust me.	CHARLES: I don't make bad decisions. I can't believe after all the years we've worked together you still don't trust me.
BRITNEY: I do trust you and you do make good decisions. I mean, sometimes you do. Oh, I don't know.	BRITNEY: I do trust you. Trust is not the issue. What I'm referring to specifically is how you make decisions during stressful times.
CHARLES: "I don't know" is right. You were the one who made last-minute changes that put us over budget! How about that for bad decision making?	CHARLES: What about how you make decisions? You're the one who went over budget with your bad decisions.
BRITNEY: You know what, you're right. I shouldn't be pointing fingers. Just ignore me. I think I'm just tired from the event.	BRITNEY: Charles, that's not fair. If you want to talk about my choices to go over budget, we can do that. But right now, I'm asking you to consider my feedback. Can you please hear me out?

(continued)

Table 7.5 *(continued)*

Message Derailed and Deflected	Compassionate Persistence
CHARLES: Yeah, thank goodness that's over. Hey, I've got some information on the Stanley project. Do you want to review it while we have time?	*CHARLES: But you're criticizing me for something I had no choice about. I had to change direction. You may not realize it but I averted an even bigger problem when I made that call. You're just upset that I didn't include you in it.*
BRITNEY: Sure, let's do that instead.	*BRITNEY: Charles, I don't know those details, but I do know this is hard to hear. I understand your pushback, but I'm really hoping we can talk openly.*
	CHARLES: Okay, say what you have to say.
	BRITNEY: As I said, I don't know all the details. I just know the outcome of last week's event was still less than ideal. I'd like to ask that, in the future, you take a few minutes to consider alternative options. And sometimes discuss it with the rest of us to help you think it through. You can still make the decision on your own.
	CHARLES: I guess that's okay. I just don't want to be bogged down with getting everyone's approval. This isn't a democracy; I have a job to do.
	BRITNEY: No democratic vote, just leveraging us as thought partners.
	CHARLES: Okay, done.

Environment

Listening to National Public Radio as I headed home one day, I heard a segment about men and vulnerability that completely and totally zeroed in on the kind of environment organizations unknowingly create that promotes avoiding honest communication, feedback, sharing, and openness. I was so mesmerized by the story that I had to pull over to the side of the road.

According to Angus Chen, NPR's host and author of *Invisibilia: How Learning to Be Vulnerable Can Make Life Safer*, men working on oil rigs in the South had become accustomed to physically and mentally tough working conditions. The men did not talk about their concerns, fears, and struggles. They did not admit when they didn't know something; instead they just tried their best to figure it out. If they made mistakes, they did their best to hide them. Some even witnessed death and dismemberment of coworkers, only to be told to get back to work without much time to mourn the loss. This was the traditional way of doing business.[5]

The story went on to describe the need for change when Shell began developing a deepwater platform, Ursa, which would become the world's deepest offshore well. Ursa's assets leader came in contact with a consultant who encouraged the company to consider addressing the emotions of the leaders and their men. In an 18-month program leading up to the deployment of teams on Ursa, men who had been conditioned their whole lives to shut up and do their jobs were asked to share their feelings and provide one another with feedback. They talked about everything from what it was like for them growing up to what it was like working with one another. The openness and honesty in giving and receiving feedback and information transformed the way the men worked together and how they lived their lives. The outcomes were amazing. A *Harvard Business Review* article, written by two professors who had studied the program and its changes to the environment, said the shift in how the men communicated with one another, especially their vulnerabilities with one another, contributed to an 84 percent decline in Shell's accident rates, and the company's level of productivity in terms of numbers of barrels, and efficiency and reliability, exceeded the industry's previous benchmark.[6]

Although Chen's story highlighted good-old-boy environments, the story reflects what happens in a range of industries from high-tech to hospitality to academic institutions. That's because creating an environment in which leaders foster open communication means leaders themselves do a good job role modeling how to receive feedback effectively.

The Feedback Trifecta—Receiving Feedback Well

When it comes to receiving feedback, the feedback trifecta still applies. Leaders lack the *courage* to listen to feedback and *skillfully* respond. As a result, leaders create an *environment* in which others are resistant to giving more feedback in the future.

Courage

Carmen is a leader who is making a shift from IT leader to executive coach. She asked me whether she could spend some time shadowing me while I'm coaching leaders. I was flattered that she would be interested in learning from me and was willing to accommodate her request. I approached a couple of my clients and got their approval to have her participate in our meetings as an observer. After each of our meetings, I asked Carmen to share her reaction to the coaching session. She shared her insights and we talked through questions she had. During one of our session debriefs, I asked Carmen whether there was anything about my approach to coaching that she would consider doing differently. No sooner had the words rolled off my tongue than she had a response. I sat a little puzzled. I had asked for feedback, but I realized as soon as I heard it that I didn't really want it. I didn't like that she actually had something specific she would do differently. I had to stop and wonder, if I didn't want feedback, why on earth did I ask for it? I realized, when I asked for feedback, I wasn't looking for critique but for validation. I wanted to know that she agreed my approach was the best approach. How dreadful to admit.

Most humans prefer validation, or at a minimum, acceptance over criticism. In their book, *Thanks for the Feedback: The Science and Art of Receiving Feedback Well*, Douglas Stone and Sheila Heen describe the need for validation and acceptance this way:

In addition to our desire to learn and improve, we long for something else that is fundamental: to be loved, accepted, and respected just as we are. And the very fact of feedback suggests that how we are is not quite okay. So we bristle: Why can't you accept me for who I am and how I am? Why are there always more adjustments and more upgrades? Why is it so hard for you to understand me? Hey boss, hey team. Hey wife, hey Dad. Here I am, this is me. Receiving feedback sits at the intersection of these two needs—our drive to learn and our longing for acceptance.[7]

Receiving feedback is complicated, and it requires courage. It requires being willing to hear someone's message when we have no idea how painful it will be. We don't know whether he or she will deliver it skillfully, minimizing the threat it represents, using empathy and exploratory language while staying compassionately persistent. Or will he or she hurl harsh words and complaints our direction, leaving only a fraction of our dignity intact? We sit bracing ourselves and doing our best not to move to reaction. Even when the other person does it skillfully, it can still sting. So it takes courage to receive feedback. The choice is ours. We don't have to receive feedback—even when we're trapped in a dreaded performance review, we could shut it out—but the consequences of avoiding it far outweigh the pain involved. This is a time we need to dig deep and find that part of us that is courageous.

Skill

Being skillful at receiving feedback means being courageous enough to hear it, acknowledge it, consider it, and determine what to do with it without moving to reaction. It doesn't mean we have to do what the other person is suggesting or that we have to agree with him or her, but it does mean that we process it thoroughly, calmly, and completely.

As referenced in Pari's story in "The Courage to Get Unstuck," Peter Senge, author of *The Fifth Discipline*, suggests that to truly be open, we can't just start a dialogue and create an environment for feedback. We need to open ourselves up to the feedback. To truly be open to feedback, we must consider "I may be wrong and the other person may be right."[8] Another scholar in the field of leadership and organization development, Peter Block, presented at a small conference I attended in Boston a few years ago. This is my recollection of what he said: "As soon as I write a book telling all of you what to think, my words become dogma and someone else should write another book telling you why I'm wrong." His intent was to convey that our knowing and understanding of reality should constantly be scrutinized. Feedback is a way to scrutinize our reality so that we can learn and grow. The question then is "How do we actually practice being open to feedback?" Here are some specific things you can do.

Set the Right Mental Framework   First, and probably the most important skill in receiving feedback, is setting the right mental framework for feedback (when you can). Go into the feedback situation knowing the inherent point of feedback is growth so that there will be constructive information provided. If you have the right mental framework in place, it can transform the way you experience receiving feedback. I relate it to going to the dentist, which is my least favorite thing to do. I put it off until the last possible minute every time and cause more problems for myself as a result. I've learned to adjust my mental framework to *There will be some pain involved; there will be some good news and some bad news about my overall dental health. The dentist will likely have recommendations for me that I won't like but I know are the right things to do, like "Floss every day."* As a result, when the visit goes as planned, or better yet, is less painful than I'd thought, I leave feeling uplifted and happy to schedule my next appointment.

Honor the Giver by Appreciating the Feedback   When feedback has been spewed on you like an exploding sewer pipe, the last thing you're likely thinking is "I'm grateful and appreciative for this feedback."

Yet, if we don't stay in a place of appreciation, we are more likely to move into reaction. We don't always have to believe the feedback, but we can be grateful that the giver was willing to be open. Feedback that goes underground through the watercooler tunnels of the workplace never seems to surface to the person who needs to hear it most. So truly, feedback from the giver can be a gift. Even if it's delivered unskillfully, and it likely will be, honoring the effort and the intent of the giver can be a powerful antidote to anger or defensiveness.

Stay in the Role of Receiver Rather than Victim Some synonyms for the word *victim* are *loser, prey, stooge, dupe, sucker, fool, fall guy, chump*, and *sap*.[9]

I don't know about you, but these are not the descriptions I want to hear about myself. Although it might feel justified, being the victim when receiving feedback puts us in a no-win scenario. Save the role of victim for times when we are actually victimized. Instead, stay in the role of receiver. Here are some synonyms for the word *receiver: recipient, beneficiary, donee*, and *the receiver of a gift*.[10] Much better, right?

One way to stay in the role of receiver is to continue asking questions of the giver. When the receiver provides information, ask questions to clarify your understanding of the feedback. Probe him or her for examples of what he or she is saying so that it is more illustrative for you. In getting curious and asking questions, you are more apt to stay open to information and more comfortable being a receiver.

All three of these techniques are supported by research that indicates our body, especially our heart, has a direct response to our emotions. For example, negative emotions, including anger, frustration, and anxiety, cause irregular and erratic heart rate patterns. As a result, when we are in this negative state, our body tends to operate inefficiently, our energy is depleted, and long-term effects produce extra wear and tear on our whole system. Conversely, positive emotions send a very different signal throughout our body. When we experience uplifting emotions, such as appreciation, joy, care, and love, our heart rhythm pattern becomes highly ordered, looking like a smooth, harmonious wave. When we are generating a harmonious heart rhythm, the body is synchronized and operates with increased efficiency and harmony. Receiving feedback well might take more work, but if we do it well, we not only grow professionally, but also actually help our body's systems synchronize and work better.

Let Yourself Mourn   During a feedback session I was leading for a team of hospital administrators, one of the leaders said, "Feedback is a lot like the mourning process. At first you're shocked, then angry, then you reject it and deny it until you finally accept it." He was right. In receiving feedback, there is a loss involved. When my friend shared the harsh feedback I mentioned earlier, it was the end of our relationship as I knew it. No matter what I chose to do with the feedback, our friendship had changed. That's the point of feedback. It moves you from one point to another in your work, your relationships, and your life. To make those transitions, you will mourn to some degree what you are leaving behind. Suppose your boss says, "I can't promote you now because you have not yet learned to delegate responsibility. You have continued to micromanage and control the environment around you regardless of the coaching I've tried to provide. I hope in time this will change, but for now my decision is made." You have a choice now to transform or stay the same while the environment around you changes. Either way, things are forever different.

As presented earlier, receiving feedback well means being willing to hear it, consider it, and then determine what to do with it. That is vastly different from our natural propensity to reject feedback and deny it when we are shocked and angry. That's why taking time to mourn first, without reacting, is so important. After you've worked through your emotions and processed the information, you can work to consider the feedback and determine how you will move to action.

Environment

When Carmen provided me with feedback on my coaching approach, I really wanted to explain why I did what I did, and I really wanted to say something mature, such as "And who are you to say anyway? Aren't you the one learning from me?" But luckily I didn't. I knew if I moved to reaction, I would close down any chance of Carmen providing me feedback in the future. I imagined that if she felt I was too sensitive, she'd likely tiptoe around me, and our engagements going forward would be awkward and less effective. That's the last thing I wanted. So I practiced being in the role of receiver rather than victim and asked lots of questions. She probably could sense something had changed for me, but I did my best anyway to make her feel comfortable continuing to share more.

When leaders move to reaction as a result of receiving feedback, they create an environment that shuts down feedback. When this happens, everyone pays for it, not just the leader. In *Primal Leadership*, Goleman, Boyatzis, and McKee describe this void of feedback as the "CEO disease."[11] The further up a leader sits in the organization, the less honest and valid the feedback that reaches him or her. As a result, the leader makes critical decisions every day based on limited and diluted information. When it comes to leadership, the most important thing leaders can do to promote healthy feedback at all levels in their organization is to receive feedback well themselves. When others have mustered up the courage to share feedback with us, how we respond will inform how—or whether—they give feedback in the future. Our response does not exist in a vacuum, either. If we react poorly, it will soon have a ripple effect through the organization as the team member shares his or her experience with others. If enough stories emerge as a pattern, then feedback ceases to exist altogether. Instead, people fall into the Big Temptation of telling the leader what he or she wants to hear (because it's easier to say) rather than what he or she needs to hear.

Chapter Application

Questions to Consider

1. How does the giving feedback trifecta apply to you?
   a. Do you find that you struggle with the courage to give feedback?
   b. Do you find that you struggle with the skills to give feedback?
   c. Do you find the environment around you promotes falling into the Big Temptation and avoiding giving feedback?
2. How does the receiving feedback trifecta apply to you?
   a. Do you find that you struggle with the courage to receive feedback well?
   b. Do you find that you struggle with the skills to receive feedback well?
   c. Do you find that you create an environment around you that encourages others to give you feedback?

Strategies to Practice

Giving Feedback

1. Minimize the threat you represent when you give feedback.
2. Use exploratory language, rather than absolutes.
3. Demonstrate compassionate persistence by not giving up on your message just because the other person doesn't like hearing what you have to say.

Receiving Feedback

1. Set the right mental framework when you can to receive feedback well.

2. Don't forget to honor the giver of feedback by sharing your appreciation for the feedback.

3. Stay in the role of receiver by asking questions and bringing more information to the conversation, rather than shutting down and becoming the victim.

Notes

1. Jung, Carl G. *Contributions to Analytical Psychology.* Translated by H. G. and Cary F. Baynes. New York: Harcourt Brace, 1928, 193.

2. Goleman, Daniel, Richard E. Boyatzis, and Annie McKee. *Primal Leadership: Realizing the Power of Emotional Intelligence.* Boston: Harvard Business School Press, 2002.

3. Losada, Marcial, and Emily Heaphy. "The Role of Positivity and Connectivity in the Performance of Business Teams: A Nonlinear Dynamics Model." *American Behavioral Scientist* 47, no. 6 (February 2004): 740–65. doi:10.1177/0002764203260208.

4. Miner, Andrew G., Theresa M. Glomb, and Charles Hulin. "Experience Sampling Mood and Its Correlates at Work." *Journal of Occupational and Organizational Psychology* 78, no. 2 (June 2005): 171–93. doi:10.1348/096317905X40105.

5. Chen, Angus. *Invisibilia: How Learning to Be Vulnerable Can Make Life Safer.* National Public Radio, June 17, 2016. http://www.npr.org/sections/health-shots/2016/06/17/482203447/invisibilia-how-learning-to-be-vulnerable-can-make-life-safer.

6. Ely, Robin J., and Debra Meyerson. "Unmasking Manly Men." *Harvard Business Review*, July–August 2008. https://hbr.org/2008/07/unmasking-manly-men

7. Stone, Douglas, and Sheila Heen. *Thanks for the Feedback: The Science and Art of Receiving Feedback Well.* New York: Penguin, 2015, 8.

8. Senge, Peter M. *The Fifth Discipline: The Art & Practice of the Learning Organization.* New York: Doubleday, 1990.

9. Lindberg, Christine A., ed. *The Oxford American Writer's Thesaurus.* Oxford, United Kingdom: Oxford University Press, 2004, 969.

10. Lindberg, *Oxford American Writer's Thesaurus*, 740.

11. Goleman, Boyatzis, and McKee, *Primal Leadership*.

8 The Courage to Be in the Middle (and Not Be in the Middle)

Be a middle who maintains your independence of thought and action in service to the system.[1]

—Barry Oshry

Elijah managed a team of programmers who loved to spend their days sitting behind a closed door, coding. His team spent little time interacting with clients or with others in the organization. Instead, Elijah spent most of his time doing that for them, and for the most part, that suited him just fine. After many years using an old enterprise system, his boss came to him with a request to update the system for their function. He gave Elijah a specific date for completion and a budget. Elijah thought the budget was a little too small and the timeline a bit too short, but he accepted the request anyway—hoping his team would be able to pull it off and maybe even surprise him with ideas for how do it with ease. After one tense and emotional meeting, Elijah discovered that his team was not at all pleased about the budget and timeline for the system upgrade. They not only believed they couldn't pull it off with the constraints but also felt it would affect other larger-priority items the company identified. They asked Elijah to go back to his boss with a list of demands, including more resources, an extended deadline, and a reprioritization of projects for the team. Unfortunately, the conversation with his boss didn't go well. Before Elijah could even present his team's demands, his superior shared further updates that actually shortened the team's deadline. When he tried to voice his concerns, Elijah was quickly shut down. He left the meeting with his head hanging low. How could he possibly go back to his team with these new terms?

Listening to this story, it's easy to think of Elijah as weak and incompetent. We wonder why he doesn't do more to support his people or stand up to his boss; and yet, at one time or another, we've all been there. We can relate to being in the middle—between our team who wants to do something one way and the boss who is directing us to do something differently. Elijah is not just in the middle in this situation; Elijah sits squarely in the middle *of the organization*.

Talk to any middle manager in any organization—for-profit, nonprofit, high-tech, healthcare—and he or she will tell you the same story. Being in the middle is rough. According to research by Bersin & Associates, things are getting increasingly difficult for middle managers.[2] Executives depend on middle managers to execute their company's vision and strategy. However, middle managers simultaneously receive fewer resources and more people to lead, and they are far less engaged than all other groups of employees. In addition, a recent study by Columbia University of nearly 22,000 full-time workers found that, compared with all other positions in the organization, middle managers were the most prone to both depression and anxiety. Researchers speculate that the tendency for middle managers to internalize failure contributes to the resulting depression.[3]

Much That Seems Personal Is Not Personal at All

Barry Oshry, researcher, author, and chief theoretical officer of Power and Systems, would agree. His own research shows that those in the middle space of organizations tend to feel that what they are experiencing is personal—and that they are failing. In fact, what they are feeling isn't personal at all, but rather, an inherent condition of being a part of a system. After decades of observing participants in systems simulations, Oshry developed a theory about organizational and system dynamics.[4]

To better understand Elijah's challenge and our own experiences when faced with these same or similar circumstances of being in the middle, we will take a deeper dive into Oshry's theory. He asserts that in any organization there are Tops—those who have overall responsibility for the organization (like Elijah's boss); there are Bottoms—those who do the work of the organization (like Elijah's team); and there are Middles (like Elijah)—who are responsible to both bottoms and tops to provide services or products to the customers (see Figure 8.1). Oshry goes on to say that in each of these spaces, there are inherent

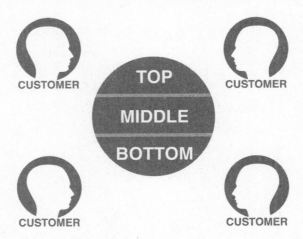

Figure 8.1 Tops, Middles, Bottoms, and Customers
Adapted from Oshry, p. xii (1995).

conditions or challenges. For Middles, that means being pulled and torn by Tops and Bottoms in different directions.

You know you've been in the middle space of organizational life if, at some point, you've felt torn between Tops and Bottoms. Maybe you felt incompetent or confused or that you weren't pleasing anyone. Sound familiar? Did you believe you were working all alone without anyone to support you? Most Middles describe these feelings as typical, and Oshry's research confirms this to be true. It's no wonder Columbia's research found Middles are the most prone to depression. This business of being in the middle is tough stuff.

Further, why should Middles feel supported when Tops and Bottoms will do whatever they can to elicit the Middles' support to their side? According to Oshry, both Tops and Bottoms will pull Middles, push them, ask them to pick sides, and question their loyalty and commitment when they don't get what they need. This makes it especially hard for Middles to express independence of thought and action. Just as we saw with Elijah, it can be challenging to take a stand when there are so many competing interests and demands that come with being a Middle (see Figure 8.2).

In the Personify Leadership program, we engage in an activity called "Lines of Communication" that simulates Top, Bottom, and Middle conditions. In this relatively brief simulation, we randomly

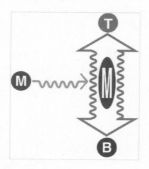

Figure 8.2 Middle Experience

Adapted from Oshry, p. 22 (1995).

select participants to serve in each role. While taking direction from Tops, Middles are charged with getting Bottoms to get the work done. Invariably, information gets lost, things get difficult, Bottoms disengage, Tops get frustrated, and Middles feel incompetent. At the end of the simulation, we point out that anyone who steps into the exercise in the Middle position experiences a similar outcome—and the outcomes are strikingly similar all over the world. This is what Oshry is referring to when he says feeling torn is not personal. It is a condition of the space that exists—with or without you. It's not about you, but rather about being in the middle of system.

System dynamics are highly underestimated in organizational life. Leaders spend so much of their time feeling as if they are failing, when in actuality, they are simply experiencing system dynamics. When they recognize they are working in gale-force winds and a Category 3 storm that started long before they entered the scene, they are far more likely to stay courageous and confident as they lead. I once led a lengthier and more complex simulation of Oshry's systems theory for a group of Middles during a retreat in Austin, Texas. One leader was so moved by the realization that she was a Middle—in a system with predictable conditions that were not personal but existed *with or without her*—she literally broke down in tears of relief. Several years later, I met with her, and she said, "That moment of realization was huge for me. I'm a completely different leader now. I trust myself more and I take more risks. I am just an all-around better leader."

According to Oshry, this leader's response is typical for a Middle—trying to please everyone and struggling to work between the Tops and Bottoms, hoping it gets better. As she learned, the Middle's *condition* is not in your control, but how you choose to respond *is* in your control. Courageous leaders make a conscious choice *not* to attempt to please everyone and hope it gets better. Instead, they leverage strategies for taking action, rather than reacting to the conditions of the system. These strategies can be uncomfortable and sometimes temporarily painful, but they provide better guidance for living and working in the middle over the long term. Let's look at a few of Oshry's strategies and how they apply in the workplace.

Be a Bottom When You Should

Although Middles sit in a precarious place in the organization, they are also closer to more valid and useful information than Tops are. You may recall the phenomenon of "CEO disease" in "The Courage to Give and Receive Feedback." Tops don't always have information they need to make informed decisions. As a result, it's common for Tops to make requests of Middles that just do not make sense for the organization. Oshry refers to this as Tops sending "stinky stuff" down a sewer pipe which backs up all over the Bottoms and Middles. An unfortunate scenario to say the least. This is where Oshry suggests that, rather than passing on instructions, decisions, or information that is flawed and toxic to Bottoms, Middles need to *be* Bottoms and create a barrier so that the flawed and toxic stuff stops with them (see Figure 8.3).

While working for a private hospitality company, I was asked by the president to make a significant cultural change. She wanted all the contract staff to work for our firm exclusively—even though the majority made their living working for multiple hospitality companies. Many of the leaders in the company strongly disagreed with the

Figure 8.3 Middle Sewer Pipe
Adapted from Oshry, p. 177 (1995).

president's vision—mostly behind closed doors and over cocktails at happy hour—and with good reason. The change meant that the contractors would be taking the risk we might not provide them enough work, whereas in the past, the safest way for them to maintain a full-time schedule was to contract with multiple companies. Most significantly, requiring contract staff to work for only one company legally changes the employee–employer relationship and results in tax implications for both the employee and the company. I advised the president of these issues, but she didn't want to hear any of it; she just wanted it done.

So, as any dutiful Middle would do, I moved forward with her request. I told my team to contact our contract staff and advise them of the requirement to sign an exclusivity contract with us. They shared the same concerns with me that I had shared with the president, and I gave them the same feedback that I had received. They left as deflated as I had felt leaving my president's office.

As you may have guessed, my staff gave it their best shot and failed. Out of 100 contract staff, only five were willing to sign the new agreement. Talk about stinky stuff! My team was drenched in it, and as a result, I lost their confidence and their trust.

When faced with a situation in which Tops lack either the integrity or insight to make informed decisions, Middles play a critical role in righting the ship. While on the surface, it may have appeared I did not have other options, the truth was I did. First, I had a team of peers who did not support this decision. I could have made an effort to rally the team and collectively share our concerns with the president, rather than going it alone. Middles are more powerful together than apart. Secondly, the buck could have stopped with me. I made no effort to research other options or present new information to my Top. I gave up my ability to influence when I chose to push down a bad decision for my team to deal with and ultimately fail at. Bottom line, I lacked the courage to be confident to do the right thing for myself, my team, and the organization.

Coach Tops to Talk with Bottoms Directly

Yaz was responsible for leading an initiative to transition employees from company-owned vehicles to a monthly car allowance policy. He thought it was a fairly straightforward change from which everyone would benefit. The employees no longer had to drive the company fleet and could select their own make and model, and the company saved significant money on insurance. It was a win-win for everyone. But that's not how the employees—Bottoms—felt. They voiced serious concerns about the change and some even threatened to quit. They told Yaz to do something about it because they weren't giving up their company cars. Yaz shared the concerns with his Top, Carlos, who said the decision was made. Yaz was stuck squarely in the middle of a mess. The closer the transition date loomed, the more the Bottoms griped and the more scared Yaz became about the potential outcome. He continued to share his concerns with his Tops, as well as any other Tops who would listen to him, but it seemed it was a done deal. Yaz thought about it and wondered whether the biggest part of the problem was that the Bottoms didn't understand the need for the change or trust the Tops' intention for the change. He had tried to explain the reasons but didn't seem to be effective. He wondered whether getting his Top in front of the Bottoms would help. Yaz shared his idea with Carlos, who as a Top, agreed it was worth a try to communicate directly with Bottoms (see Figure 8.4).

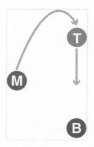

Figure 8.4 Tops Communicate Directly to Bottoms

Adapted from Oshry, p. 181 (1995).

In an empathetic and transparent address to the Bottoms during an on-site visit, Carlos explained the company rationale behind the decision to shift from car to allowance. He shared the benefits for the company, saying, "Yes, it is true; the company does benefit, and so do you." He went on to describe the advantages of the change to the Bottoms, which did seem to settle some concerns. Those who still had doubts asked questions and aired their frustrations, to which Carlos responded honestly and openly. In the end, Carlos was able to calm most of their fears and gain necessary support for the change.

What Yaz did in this scenario took great courage. Rather than continue to be in the Middle of the Tops and Bottoms on an issue that was hugely significant and controversial, he stepped out of the middle and coached his Top to talk with Bottoms directly. The outcome was far more productive than if he had continued to be the Middle, sharing information back and forth. Granted, Middles aren't always able to step out and facilitate Tops and Bottoms working together directly, but in situations where it matters most—and where other efforts have failed—it is not only courageous, but also highly effective.

Build a Support System with Other Middles

Being in the middle is lonely. Most Middles see themselves as disconnected from other Middles. They either assume they don't need one another to thrive or think they wouldn't understand one another's worlds if they broke out of their silos and worked together. And yet, what Oshry's research has found is that "Middle Integration" is a fundamental strategy for success.

You may recall David, the leader whom I said I would follow off a cliff if he asked me to. Luckily he never did, but he did ask me to assist him in creating collaboration across his senior leadership team. David's vision was that his direct reports—who represented various regions across the United States—would work together as peers to lead the overall organizational goals. He empowered them to set strategy, execute it, and make critical decisions on behalf of the organization. He gave them resources and tools; he brought them together on multiple occasions to share his vision for the team; and he created an environment in which they could partner together to reach a greater result than if they worked apart. Unfortunately for David, this vision was never fully realized. Members of the team had dramatically different styles and opinions—which perhaps could have been harnessed to produce creativity and innovation, but ultimately were not. Instead, the group bickered and fought. During one team meeting (which included an off-site dinner) with these Middles, I asked what I thought was a simple question. I wanted to know their perspective on a recent change request from the corporate office. I had no idea what a firestorm I had just ignited. Within minutes, the discussion among the Middles became explosive. I finally excused myself and headed home. To this day, I'm pretty sure no one from that team was aware I even left. I asked a colleague the next day how the evening ended, and she shared that they continued arguing, eventually leaving the dinner one by one. This team of Middles was in shambles.

Oshry says those in the middle space of organizational life tend to see themselves as unique, having little in common with one another. Middles are typically competitive and evaluative of one another, thus creating interpersonal tension, and they are likely unaware of the possibilities of their collective power. When Middles continue to operate from this mind-set, they struggle to integrate and miss the opportunities integration brings to them and the organization. These characteristics, as Oshry describes, show how Middles tend to operate: in silos and dispersed. (See Figure 8.5.)

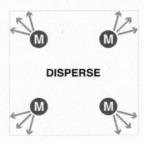

Figure 8.5 Middles Dispersed

Adapted from Oshry, p. 160 (1995).

Conversely, I had the great privilege of working with another team of Middles who demonstrated the ability not only to collaborate but also to establish an incredible support system with one another. Together they shared resources, set strategy, executed well, and held one another and their teams accountable. They were the personification of David's vision for his Middles team and Oshry's research on Middles integration. (See Figure 8.6.)

Recently, I had the opportunity to interview this well-integrated team as a group. Here are some of the things I heard from these Middles about how they came to form such a supportive team and the ensuing benefits that followed.

> "We just said, 'Look, we are going to choose to trust one another,' and we do trust one another in everything we do."

> "We operate as a peer team, regardless of how our roles or hierarchy have changed over time. Now, I have previous peers reporting to me, but that doesn't change how we work together."

> "When I joined this peer team, I had an in-it-for-myself mentality. But I wanted what they had, so I worked to change my mindset to be a part of the team."

> "We know we need one another to get things done, and it's usually faster to just reach out and say, 'Hey, I've got a problem.

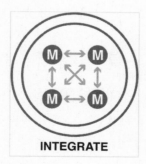

Figure 8.6 Middles Integrating

Adapted from Oshry, p. 160 (1995).

Can you help me solve it?' or 'Can you take a look at this e-mail before I send it?' We've always been looking to one another for support, regardless of how our leadership has changed over time, or any other organizational changes."

"We are brutally honest with one another about feedback. Everything is on the table."

"We lean on one another in the areas we don't have strengths."

"Part of why our collaboration continues is we know we have a lot more influence as a group than we do individually."

"We have moved our team members from one team to another because we can communicate and work through things with one another, whereas other groups would need their manager to get involved to make these decisions."

"We look at what's in the best interests of the other person and helping them grow—it's not just about what's best for our collective goal. We ask one another, 'Where do you want your career to go, and how can I help you achieve it?'"

Integrating with other Middles takes courage, because it requires being vulnerable. You have to be open to others' ideas and criticism, allow yourself to ask for help, risk individual success for team success, and be willing to be humble and support others, instead of just yourself and your team. Integrating brings forth far more strength and results—not only for the Middle but also for the entire organization. It is an example of bigger-purpose–seeker courage in action. As you've heard in the above quotes from a team of integrated Middles, the benefits far outweigh the risk and the pain in getting started. Oshry says, "Middles think the reason they don't integrate is because of how they feel about one another, and if they felt differently about one another, then they would integrate. In reality, it's the other way around. They feel the way they feel about one another because they *don't* integrate, and if they did integrate, they would feel very differently" (emphasis in original).[5]

Middle Between Two Ends

Being in the middle space of organizational life is not the only time we feel torn as Middles. As a matter of fact, no matter what space we occupy—Top, Middle, or Bottom—we can find ourselves in the middle. Oshry describes the Middle between two ends as the "dance of blind reflex." When we find ourselves in the middle of two ends who have the ability to solve their own problems but use us—the Middle—to do it for them, we are now in the midst of the tango. You don't have to think long before you can imagine your own examples in which you have done this dance: Middle between direct boss and dotted-line boss, Middle between your spouse and your parent, Middle between the customer and the Bottom, and Middle between two feuding friends or employees. The list is truly endless.

Oshry describes a gradual breakdown that happens in relationships where responsibility reflexively lies with the Middle, not the ends. In the short term, this arrangement may appear productive, but when things go wrong, the Middle gets blamed—reinforcing the stigma of Middles being incompetent and weak. More important, it reinforces how we *feel* in the middle space—incompetent and weak. In the long term, the result of being the Middle between two ends is nearly always fatal to both the Middle and the ends. If responsibility continues to fall on the Middle, the result is burnout and resentment for the Middle and dependency on the Middle by the ends. When two ends become dependent on a Middle, they become unable to solve their own problems (see Figure 8.7).

Let's look at some of these middle-between-two-ends relationships where burnout and disablement result.

Figure 8.7 Middle Between Two Ends

Adapted from Oshry, p. 100 (1995).

Disabling Others to Solve Their Own Problems

Kim is a strong leader who values people and a peaceful environment. In "The Courage to Take a Stand," I referenced Kim's early childhood experiences that helped shape her values for peace and harmony. Her values have driven her to create a thriving career. In her nonprofit, her city has outperformed every other like-sized city for three years running. After tremendous growth, Kim decided to hire a new director, Roxanne, for the city location and promote the previous director, Brett, to a national role overseeing the execution of the city's strategy. This meant Brett and Roxanne would be working closely together during the transition, and with the ongoing advisement and direction of the location.

Unfortunately, before Kim could blink an eye, Brett and Roxanne were in a dispute over how to lead the city location. At first, she didn't think much of it. Brett had been a very successful director, and Kim had predicted it would be difficult for him to pass the baton to Roxanne. Roxanne's approach to leading the city was markedly different. Brett argued that he had set up a well-oiled machine and there was no reason to change a thing, while Roxanne looked at the city location as a blank canvas and was gearing up for creativity and innovation. The two butted heads on a number of occasions. Of course, when this happened, they would go to Kim. Usually one at a time, each voicing his or her concerns about the other. Kim, the ultimate peacemaker, would spend countless hours coaching them to see the other person's perspective. When that didn't work, she would step in and do some of the work for them or redirect the work to other team members in an attempt to calm the escalating tension between Brett and Roxanne.

It wasn't until I sat down with Kim and discussed the situation that she began to see that she was the Middle between two ends. Brett and Roxanne rarely spoke. If anything, they actively avoided one another. Kim was responsible for relaying concerns and sharing feedback, while problem solving to keep the city location moving forward. Unwittingly, Kim was enabling bad behavior and ultimately disabling them from learning to solve their own problems. The longer she stayed in the middle, the more comfortable Brett and Roxanne became with leveraging Kim as their problem solver. This, in turn, prevented Brett and Roxanne from doing the real work of learning to communicate, problem solve, and deal effectively with each other. After realizing this, Kim decided to step out of the middle and facilitate Brett and Roxanne's working together. It was a painful start, but over time, the two learned to work together to solve their own problems, rather than involving Kim. It wasn't perfect, but it was a move in the right direction.

Playing the Mediator

When I first met Albert, he raved about his team member Jessica and shared how frustrated he was with another team member, Lynnette. The three had been working together for a very long time. They knew one another well and knew what to expect from one another. Because Albert had come to anticipate that he and Lynnette would not agree and things would get touchy quickly, he started going to Jessica to get things done. Jessica was amicable, friendly, and easy to work with. What fascinated me about watching their interactions was that no one else seemed to see an issue. Lynnette enjoyed not having to work with Albert directly, Albert was happy not working directly with Lynnette, and Jessica prided herself on being able to mediate the two. The problem was the business was growing, and as it did, it became more obvious the way in which they were working together was no longer working for the business. Jessica was feeling overwhelmed, playing the messenger and constantly tiptoeing around the issues with both Albert and Lynnette. She became more and more frustrated with the weight the extra mediation responsibility was creating. She realized that, as much as she loved being in the middle, she was also starting to resent it.

Jessica and I worked together to establish appropriate boundaries for her and Lynnette and for her and Albert. Instead of being torn in the middle, she practiced stepping out and coaching Lynnette and

Albert to deal with each other directly. The effort was a success. Of course, no later had she made this transition than a new employee, Marcy, started. Marcy also struggled with Lynnette. In a meeting I was facilitating between Lynnette and Marcy, Jessica started to step in to explain Lynnette's intention to Marcy and vice versa. I stopped Jessica and pointed out how she was stepping into the middle again. She was blown away. "Wow," she said, "I really didn't see how natural this role has become for me."

Being a mediator is a fantastic role to play—when your role is to mediate. When your role is to *lead*, it's rarely productive. Many leaders buy into the myth that it's their responsibility to solve people's problems for them, especially for their direct reports. I've heard leaders say, "It's my job to ensure my people get along." The reality is it's not your role as a leader to solve problems two people are having or to ensure they get along; rather, it's your job to surface the issues and hold them accountable. That looks a bit different. Likely something more like this comment of a middle leader to two feuding employees:

> Look, I see that there is an issue between the two of you. I'm not sure what the root cause is or how to fix it, but I do want it solved. As you know, on our team we value transparency and teamwork. Your behaviors toward one another do not reflect either of these values. I would like for the two of you to discuss—with each other—the challenges you have and how you plan to solve them. Afterward, I'd like for you to share with me what you agreed to. I'll be happy to hold you accountable to the outcome you've committed to with each other, but keep in mind each of you will need to hold the other accountable to the commitments of how you will behave and act differently to get to that outcome. Now, any questions about how to proceed?

Being Caught Between Two Bosses

Toward the end of my tenure as an internal company leader, I was hired by an exceptionally smart and caring leader, a divisional president, to be his vice president of organization and leadership development. He had a compelling vision for the role in his growing division, and I was incredibly excited to be part of it. Shortly after taking the position, I was introduced to the senior vice president of human resources for the corporate group, and we developed a strong dotted-line relationship. I met many other members of the corporate leadership team, including the chief operating officer (COO), and I quickly realized that most of the leadership within our division was far removed from the corporate office. To say the division worked in a silo was an understatement. My gesture to connect with corporate and strengthen the alliance between the two groups was genuinely appreciated by the head office, but at the same time, was mildly distasteful for my boss.

Within months of this attempted bridging, I found myself the Middle between two ends. The senior vice president of HR reached out to me with some news and a request. He said the COO was planning to make a change with my boss. They had already found his replacement but needed my help to set up the transition. I was asked to meet with the soon-to-be leader and brief him in advance on the status of the talent in the organization. I was instructed to work with him to prepare the follow-on meeting that would occur directly after my boss was transitioned to another position and the new leader was introduced.

In some respects, the role I was asked to play was customary for an HR leader; however, the dynamics of being responsible for the transition of your boss out of his role were not. It felt awkward and uncomfortable. For days, I struggled with what to do, how to handle the information I had that no one else did, and how I felt about being in the middle. On one hand, I felt honored corporate trusted me to assist in such an important change; on the other hand, I felt deceptive and disloyal. In the end, I did what was asked of me and assisted our corporate group in the transition. Directly following the transition, I felt sick to my stomach and hugely disappointed in myself. I called my now previous boss to apologize, but he let my call go to voicemail and refused my calls for weeks. Needless to say, I did not honor the courageous leader in me in this situation.

Being the Middle between two ends can feel like dancing between two people in a swordfight. It requires tremendous agility to be effective, and in the end, someone is still likely to get hurt. It's a no-win proposition. The solution is to find ways to connect the ends and work yourself out of a role. Of course, this requires courage for many reasons:

- We like to be in control. Why empower others when we can control the outcome by doing it ourselves?

- It makes us feel important to be in the middle. Why teach others to solve their own problems when we can solve things for them?

- We like the information we get being in the middle. Why share information when we have power as the recipient and disseminator of important information?

Stepping out of the Middle

When you are ready to give up the power, information, and control that comes with middle space, connecting two ends together is as simple as facilitating the two you are standing between to come together. Instead of being in the middle of all things, you are in the middle of some, while facilitating most things. It's a huge time-saver and a great way to develop others. If you think back to "The Courage to Delegate," connecting two ends is a fantastic strategy for getting out of the Delegation Doom Loop.

I once contracted with a private company in Montana that required I be on-site working with a leadership team one week a month for six months. I would fly in Sunday night, work in the office with the team all week, and fly home on Friday. At first, I was a little lost about how to get things done, but being as resourceful as I am, I located a helpful soul right away: the leadership team's executive administrator, Colleen. She was great! I would go to her for just about everything—to scan documents, order lunch, change my reservations, locate a company car, schedule a location visit, find my way to the restroom—you name it.

At first Colleen was very accommodating, but it became apparent over time that my resourcefulness had become her additional workload. So, gracefully, Colleen started to introduce me to other tools and resources besides herself. I would go to her for a scan, and she showed me how to download an application on my phone to allow me to do all the scanning myself. Instead of ordering my lunch, she gave me menus and contact information for restaurants nearby. She stopped putting herself in the middle but also facilitated my connecting directly with the resources and people I needed during each of my trips. Colleen continued to be a great resource for others and me; however, because she took herself out of the middle of the unnecessary roles I had originally requested of her, she was far more capable of doing the important things that others and I needed of her. I've often thought about Colleen and how much other leaders could learn from her and her respectful ability to facilitate herself out of the middle when she stood between two people or a person and a resource that needed to be connected.

Middle Space and Courage

As we've witnessed through these stories, there is discomfort, pain, and struggle in the middle. Some of it is necessary, and some of it is not. Consider this: Maybe the pain associated with learning when to be in the middle, when to step out of the middle, or how to navigate the middle space when you have no control over being there is exactly the point. Leaders in the middle feel lost and endure darkness for the sole purpose of learning to see. As we already know, Pain + Meaning = Growth. It's during this time, in the middle, that leaders learn how to give their experiences powerful meaning. They can choose to be

victims and assign the meaning that life is out of their control.
Or they can choose to be courageous leaders who embrace the meaning that life is what you choose to do with the things out of your
control. This meaning prepares them for executive-level humility,
presence, confidence, and composure—the paradoxical mix of characteristics that Jim Collins refers to in his Level 5 leadership definition.[6]
Great leaders evolve from the middle.

Chapter Application

Questions to Consider

1. Do you find yourself taking things personally when they are
   not about you but potentially about the system? If so, what
   in this chapter is helpful in changing your perspective?
2. What are some examples of where you feel you are experiencing the middle condition?
3. What are some strategies that you find useful for being
   more effective in the middle? If you were to apply those
   strategies to your real-world experiences, how do you think
   you and your team might benefit?
4. Where do you find yourself struggling as a Middle between
   two ends?
   a. What's the impact of this for you and the ends?
   b. Is this a situation you want to change? If so, how do
      you plan to do this?

Strategies for Being in the Middle

1. Be a Bottom when you should. Don't just pass along your
   Top's message if you don't agree. Sort out where you and
   your Top differ before taking action you may not endorse.

2. Coach Tops to talk with Bottoms directly on issues that are best communicated from Tops, such as strategic initiatives, touchy subjects that require support, or areas that you feel Bottoms may be the most resistant to.

3. Integrate with your peers (other Middles) by meeting regularly without your Top. Find ways you can support one another and the organization by working together.

4. Get out of the middle between two ends when you find yourself enabling bad behavior or disabling others to do things for themselves.

Notes

1. Oshry, Barry. *Seeing Systems: Unlocking the Mysteries of Organizational Life.* San Francisco: Berrett-Koehler, 1995. Used with kind permission.

2. Garr, Stacia. "Maximizing Middle Managers: Four Practices to Drive Business Results." Bersin. October 19, 2011. https://www.bersin.com/Practice/Detail.aspx?id=14740.

3. Prins, Seth J., Lisa M. Bates, Katherine M. Keyes, and Carles Muntaner. "Anxious? Depressed? You Might Be Suffering from Capitalism: Contradictory Class Locations and the Prevalence of Depression and Anxiety in the USA." *Sociology of Health & Illness* 37, no. 8 (November 2015): 1352–72.

4. Oshry, *Seeing Systems.*

5. Oshry, *Seeing Systems.*

6. Collins, Jim. *Good to Great: Why Some Companies Make the Leap … and Others Don't.* New York: HarperBusiness, 2001.

9 Grow, Recover, Repeat

Courage doesn't always roar. Sometimes courage is the quiet voice at the end of the day saying, "I will try again tomorrow." [1]

—Mary Anne Radmacher

I'm a runner. I get up almost every morning before the sun, lace up my tennis shoes, and hit the pavement. I run a 6-mile loop that takes me on a beautiful journey through the intercoastal parks of Fort Lauderdale and down A1A Boulevard with the ocean to my side. I don't consider myself religious, but when it comes to running, I am a devotee. Running is my ritual. I realize for the nonrunners reading this, it may sound a little crazy rather than serene, but I promise you: for me it is my bliss. For years, I'd run countless miles without any injuries until six months ago, when an incident halted my bliss and replaced it with pain.

At first I could still run. So I did. For the next two months, I ignored the pain that set in each time I dove into my first mile. I felt it, but I was able to push past it. Although enduring physical pain is not really my thing, my desire to run was greater than my desire to stop the pain. In fact, as we've explored throughout this book, that is what courage is all about—moving to action in the face of pain. So I deduced that continuing was necessary. A few weeks after my injury, I laced up and began my normal morning run, but I just couldn't do it. The pain had gotten so severe I was almost limping. I couldn't take one more step.

After an examination, my doctor diagnosed a trigger point spasm in my left glute. Although a trigger point is not that serious, untreated, the pain can be excruciating. Trigger points occur when a runner does not appropriately recover after a long or intense period of exercise, creating muscular overload. There are simple things I could have done daily to help prevent the injury. The fact that I ignored my injury and ran despite it made my situation far worse.

Pain is always meant to be temporary, not permanent. Once you build muscle memory through pain, you can do the exact same activity and feel little to no pain. It's only when you take your exertion to the next level that you feel pain again. This is normal. Pain that goes on and on without end is not normal. It's an indication that you need to stop, recover, and heal or that you need to change something in your life (see "The Courage to Get Unstuck").

Despite hoping for a quick solution to my condition, what I got instead was a prescription for no running until my muscle returned to its normal state of health. In the world of courageous leadership, returning to a normal state of health is also important to lace up and make our next courageous move.

This concept doesn't just apply to athletes. Almost every living thing goes through a cycle that moves from growth to recovery to growth again. In plant life, flowers and trees bloom in the spring and summer months and then begin their recovery in the fall and winter months only to start the process of blooming again in the spring. Some animals hunt, gather, and play in the spring, summer, and fall months but hibernate in the winter months. The ocean tides pull in toward the ocean and then sprawl out toward the shore daily. The sun rises in the morning and sets at night. There is a rhythm to this moving outward to grow and then moving inward to renew that is a necessary part of life.

In leadership, recovery is also necessary. It's an important part of what maintains a leader's stamina. This business of courage is not easy. Whether it's a humbling experience, giving or receiving tough feedback, delegating, taking a stand, or any other form of courage, when we have completed the task of moving to action in the face of pain, the next most valuable thing we can do for ourselves is to stop and recover. It's during this time of recovery that we make sense of our pain and explore meaning (Pain + Meaning = Growth).

Recovery in the Workplace

Chris is a vice president of information technology for a department that supports multiple privately held companies. He oversees a team of six managers who lead a combined team of 45 global IT professionals. During my first coaching session with Chris, I shared results from the 360-degree feedback assessment completed by his peers, boss, customers, and direct reports. The report highlighted one major problem: In general, people who worked with and for Chris did not trust him. Chris was concerned about this feedback and immediately honed in on his direct report team. We agreed it would be helpful if I met with his team to talk through some of their specific concerns about Chris's leadership. I spent an hour with his team as they outlined multiple incidents of mistrust and grievances they had with him over the years. They truly wanted to see a change and were desperate to do whatever it took to make that happen. I agreed I would do my best to assist Chris with his part, but I also reminded them they had a role as well. Before adjourning, they agreed to do what was in their control to change, and I agreed to share their feedback with Chris.

A little over a year later, Chris described our conversation this way.

> The weekend you called me to share the team's feedback was one of the most jarring times of my life. I don't remember anything else

about that weekend except talking to you. After we spoke, I didn't know if I would recover or not. The feedback was so surprising and different than I thought it would be. During our conversation, I wrote six pages of notes. I still have those pages folded up in the desk drawer of my office at home and every once in a while, I take it out and read it, partly as a celebration of changing and growing but also as a reminder of what's possible when you don't keep growing.

In fact, Chris has grown to become an even stronger leader today than ever before. Two years later, people who meet him now are amazed to find out that he ever had trust issues with others. It's almost impossible to find a single bit of untrustworthiness residue anywhere near him. Now, his team performs at an even higher level and is a self-described family.

Indications We Need Recovery

Chris initially described his response to his experience as anger and victimization. He said it was easier to believe that others were holding him to a higher standard than what they were holding themselves to. He also thought it was unfair that he was part of a challenging environment, and it was really the culture around him, not his behaviors, that made leading tough. Just as I had felt in my recovery whenever I saw a runner passing by, Chris felt resentment building up in him.

Here are some indicators that you might be ready to move to the recovery phase before continuing on your courageous journey.

1. Your body is showing signs of physical breakdown and stress.
2. You feel overwhelmed, in despair, and void of meaning.
3. Your feelings continue to drive you to *reaction* versus action.
4. You regularly worry about the future and fixate on past mistakes.
5. You dread having to meet daily challenges.

6. You have increased using strategies to numb your pain, such as drugs, alcohol, food, sex, or any other kind of stimulant or depressant.

7. You perceive stressful situations as largely out of your control.

Chris's Story of Recovery

It's fair to say when you listen to Chris's story, he was demonstrating some of these indicators and was in need of recovery. For Chris, recovery came in many forms over time, which is generally true for most of us. In my conversation with Chris, here are some of the methods he shared that helped him make the transition from his Humbling Experience to the strong, vibrant leader he is today.

Let Go of Control

My first step of recovery came from realizing that I could only change what I could control. I think for so long I had been trying to control so many things. What I figured out was the only thing I could work on was me. I realized letting go of control was the catalyst for my own change. I had to stop fighting for my interpretation of the situation. I just chose one day to focus only on what I can control. That was the day I really started leading.

Get Guidance and Support from Others

As soon as I hung up the phone with you I told my wife everything. She said, "They know a different Chris than I do. Don't worry, you'll get through this." I also had my faith and I knew that meant I had a choice about who I wanted to be in this situation. I chose to work toward being a servant leader. You helped me a lot with this as my coach and so did a couple of other mentors and coworkers I could trust to turn to.

We all need people to turn to when we are in recovery. Dr. Brené Brown defines *connection* as "the energy that exists between two people when they feel seen, heard, and valued; when they can give and receive without judgment; and when they derive sustenance and strength from the relationship."[2] It's important when we are looking for guidance and support during recovery that we look for people who meet this definition because being a courageous leader doesn't mean doing it all alone. During an important annual event for Personify Leadership, our team member and friend, Linda, was on-site working hard while dealing with extremely difficult personal circumstances. When I asked her how she was managing to stay focused and hold it all together, she shared with me a powerful saying that she learned from two of her dear friends. "Be brave. And holler if you need me."[3] Linda explained that, for her, the strength to be brave is possible because there are supportive, caring people whom she can call on when she needs them. Although no one could change what she was going through, knowing she could "holler" when she needed us allowed Linda to find her courage.

Go Easy on Yourself and Take Your Time

> As part of our coaching, you had introduced me to another leader who had a similar struggle in his career. One of the things I took away from my conversation with that leader was that change wouldn't happen overnight. I actually took some comfort in knowing this would take time. The mechanics that had gotten me into my situation didn't happen overnight and so getting out of the hole I had dug myself in would also take some time. I've always been a person who is okay with the journey as long as I know where I'm going. So that gave me some peace, and I needed that peace to keep me moving.

It's important as you recover that you don't expect too much from yourself. Like Chris, we all need time to return to our optimal performance, especially when we are making critical changes, as he did. He would have been setting himself up for failure if he had expected anything more of himself.

Going easy on yourself and taking time to recover can also mean giving yourself a break. Let yourself relax a little and remember to breathe! It's also important to give yourself some time off. If you need a day away from the office or an afternoon on the golf course or at the spa—do it! I had a friend recently experience a major setback professionally. Instead of pushing herself to the brink, she took a personal day for herself. She probably deserved more than a day, but at least she gave herself that when most often we keep driving to the next thing. When I need time off, I usually block a morning for the kids and me to go to the beach, or I'll go shopping with a friend. Regardless of what works for you, it's important you have something that helps you wind down after your stressful event.

Recovery Is a Team Effort

I knew in order for me to change, the team would need to give me a chance. That meant that it wasn't just me in recovery but the team was in recovery too. We had to pull back and figure out how to work in the same space again. I had hope, though, because I actually figured if the team had the courage to share their candid feedback then there probably was a commitment for them to change if I changed. I definitely had to lead; I had to do my part first, but they came around to do their part too. When I did get it right, it built confidence in myself and in the process. We were honest enough with each other to know that there would be ups and downs in that journey. We went on a ledge together. Somewhere after about six months to a year, it started moving so fast. Now we have so much velocity I can't even imagine we were ever there two years ago.

Returning to a normal state as a team (recovering as a team) requires that everyone involved takes time to heal and recover personally first and then do his or her part to recover his or her working relationships. One of the most rewarding things about working with Chris and his team during this transition was observing them all move through this process. In the end, they were all committed to doing what needed to be done for the team's success. Chris and his team worked hard to achieve this; it wasn't just luck. Not all teams have the guts and wherewithal to make these kinds of transitions. They get stuck in anger and victimization largely because they don't take time to recover and heal before expecting to be fully functional again. If a team moves back into day-to-day operations too quickly without honoring their pain, they are more likely to repeat the pattern that got them into the problem in the first place. The same is true for one-on-one relationships, not just team dynamics. Anytime we need forgiveness (to give or receive) and healing in a relationship, time for recovery is necessary.

Use Humor

> Once the team and I started to make progress on our working relationships, we started using humor a lot more. Not barbed humor in a passive-aggressive way but more the don't-take-yourself-so-seriously kind of way. The team would kind of make fun of me when I'd start falling back into old behaviors, saying things like, "Hey, Chris, you're starting to remind me of the guy we almost voted off the island." This kind of humor is about being fallible and embracing our humanity. As a team, we know each other's strengths and weaknesses. Sometimes when we laugh at ourselves and give others permission to laugh at us, we are reminded that we belong to something bigger than ourselves. We are all in it together and we will work to support each other and compensate for each other. Not to mention, when we laugh together, it's a great way to let off some steam.

Research shows that humor increases engagement, improves productivity, increases happiness, reduces stress, and strengthens the immune system. It doesn't hurt that it has also been shown to burn calories. But most important for teams, humor builds connection. When teams use humor as Chris described, it can help reinforce progress they've already made and keep them enjoying one another's company even during tough times. As Chris mentions, barbed humor, on the other hand, is passive-aggressive humor, which undermines the team's progress. Using humor to convey a message when it should be a courageous discussion is very different from using humor as a way to heal.

Teresa's Story of Recovery

Teresa A. Taylor, former chief operating officer of Qwest Telecommunications and author of *The Balance Myth*, spoke with me about what it was like for her to lead as an executive and be a mom of two sons.[4] Teresa is a believer in integrating all parts of yourself, rather than trying to balance life. For her, this is how she learned to recover quicker and face more leadership challenges head on.

Find Your Pattern of Success Every couple of years or so at Qwest, Teresa would be promoted. At first, the news would be welcomed and usually included a celebration dinner with her family. Shortly after, however, panic and self-doubt would set in. Typically, Teresa was the one sent into a department to clean up messes, so rarely did she receive a promotion that came without a unique set of challenges. Probably her scariest experience was taking over the human resources department, which she described as completely out of her wheelhouse. On the first day in her new role, four employees resigned.

> Once I got past the panic, I thought, *All right, I know how to do this. I know how to assess a team. I know how to develop people.* So I started doing what I already knew best. I already had a pattern that worked for me in the past, and rather than create more stress, I would rely on that pattern.

Let Yourself Express Emotions Appropriately Teresa admitted that once in a while, when things got too overwhelming for her, she would excuse herself from a meeting, go to the bathroom, and cry. A woman who is both accomplished and sophisticated made no bones about it. For her, crying was a way to recover.

I'm a big crier! I wouldn't just break down in a meeting. That wouldn't be appropriate and would make everyone else uncomfortable, but I would leave the meeting and head to the bathroom. I was only one of two women on the floor so it was no big deal to go in there and cry. We kept makeup and tissue on hand for just that purpose. Then I'd head back into the meeting and move on.

Simplify Things   For Teresa, fundamentally, one of the most important things that came from her life experience—having it all at work and at home—was to find ways to simplify her life. When she simplified things more, Teresa needed less recovery, so when she found herself in need of recovery, it was usually because something required simplicity.

The way I took care of myself during those really busy times was to simplify and narrow my focus. That meant prioritizing where I spent my time and what was important. For example, if I decided to be at a business meeting instead of with my kids, then I needed to be at that event and not feel guilty but instead be present. If I chose to be at a dinner with girlfriends rather than a work dinner, I would be with my friends and not be checking my phone. I stayed focused on the choice I made. It was easier than trying to take on the world, and it allowed me to enjoy all the parts of my life.

Earlier in "The Courage to Be Humble," I shared one of my more profound Humbling Experiences, when I broke down in tears in front of a group I was leading after receiving tough feedback. Later that day, I remember (uncharacteristically) walking up to the bar at the airport and ordering a shot and a beer. I slept during the whole flight home, hoping I didn't have to wake up—ever. My husband was at the airport to greet me, and when I finally had the courage to tell him what had happened, he was very comforting. The next day he bought a small sign and hung it next to my bathroom sink. It reads: "Simplify." Like Teresa, I found recovery during a painful period in my career by slowing down and setting priorities. I had lost focus of what was important and created a mess for myself because of it. Simplifying wasn't just a strategy I adopted; over time, it has also become a way of living.

Build a Network   Just like Chris and Linda, Teresa finds comfort in her family and friends, as well as in the social networks around her.

> I'm a firm believer in women's groups and having a good group of women to support you in your life. I always had a women's networking group that I belonged to where I attended regular events. Whether formal or informal, lunches or cocktail hours with someone outside of my company was the best way for me to step out—literally—walk down the street and get away from my day.

There are many ways to recover and they are largely personal. Everyone heals and rejuvenates in his or her own way. What worked for Chris and Teresa may not be what works for you. Finding your path to recovery is an important part of being a courageous leader.

In leadership and in life, recovery is what brings us the insight and strength to continue on our courageous journey. When we minimize our pain with the intention to heal and rejuvenate, we give ourselves the necessary tools to maintain courageous leadership. Without recovery, we will burn out and, more significant, suffer without the benefit of meaning and transformation.

Chapter Application

Questions to Consider

1. When reviewing the indications we need recovery, do you find you are experiencing any of these regularly? If so, do you need to take time to recover?
2. What are the ways in which you find you recover? What strategies have you used in the past that work well for you?
3. Do you see others around you who show signs of needing recovery? If so, how might you support them in their recovery?

(continued)

(continued)

Strategies for Recovery

1. Practice letting go of control of the things you perceive are in your control yet truly may not be.
2. Seek guidance and support from others around you. If you don't have a support system, make it your first priority to create one. Asking for help is a great way to practice the courage to be humble.
3. Go easy on yourself and take your time in the recovery process. If you can, delay any major changes or initiatives that will require running at full speed again until you are ready.
4. Use humor as a way to soothe pain and rebuild relationships.
5. Find appropriate ways to express your emotions, rather than suppress them during your stressful and difficult times of recovery.
6. Simplifying your life to make things easier for you will eliminate unnecessary struggling in the future.

Notes

1. Radmacher, Mary Anne. *Courage Doesn't Always Roar.* San Francisco: Conari Press, 2009. Used with permission from Red Wheel Weiser, LLC.
2. Brown, Brené. *The Gifts of Imperfection: Let Go of Who You Think You're Supposed to Be and Embrace Who You Are.* Center City, MN: Hazelden Publishing, 2010. Reprinted with permission.
3. In memory of P. K. Worley and Brenda Worley Billings.
4. Taylor, Teresa A. *The Balance Myth: Rethinking Work-Life Success.* Austin, TX: Greenleaf Book Group Press, 2013.

10 Big Dreams, Big Moves

If your dream doesn't scare you it's not big enough.[1]

—Muhammad Ali

I started my first business when I was six months pregnant with my first child. Before I made the move to leave my comfy, well-paid job as an executive to become an entrepreneur, I called every woman I knew who had started her own business (the list was much shorter than I would wish). Each shared valid reasons to consider staying in my corporate role while starting out as a mom. They shared their stories of surprises that come up during pregnancy, parenting, and running a business. They talked about low levels of energy, struggles with postpartum, the desire to be home with the children rather than working, the lag time between start-up and profitability, and the stresses of being an entrepreneur. I listened to all of them and their valuable insight, but in the end, decided to start my business anyway. Some might call me a little crazy, yet I knew that, for myself, the freedom to be my own boss while being a first-time mom was the combination that worked best for me.

As it turns out, I did struggle with most of the challenges they warned me of, and yet I've never regretted my decision—not even for a single day. Now, almost seven years later, I couldn't imagine my life any other way. The decisions I made then have propelled me into a completely different place in life, one that is far more aligned with my dreams. I'm aware that my dreams were unconventional, but they were mine. I embraced them and lived them fully.

Big Dreams

If you asked a random group of people whether they were living the Big Dreams they had for themselves when they left high school or college, most would answer no. Staffing agency Kelly Services reported in its 2013 Global Workforce Index (KGWI) survey of 120,000 respondents from 31 countries that a shocking 48 percent of workers are unhappy in their current jobs.[2]

I think it's safe to assume most people either have abandoned their dreams for one reason or another or embraced their dreams but got stuck somewhere along the way. My sister is one of those people. She wanted to be a comedian; instead, she is the funniest accountant I know. She regrets very little, but that doesn't keep her from still dreaming about opening for Chris Rock or hosting the Oscars. And who knows, maybe she still will one day. I know if she did, I'd be there jumping up and down like an idiot, waving a huge banner that said, "That's my little sister!"

To achieve a Big Dream, we have to set big goals. To achieve big goals, we have to make Big Moves. To make Big Moves, we need to be courageous. Not just any kind of courage, but all facets of courage. And not just some of the time, but most of the time. That means choosing discomfort and pain over comfort and ease *most of the time*. Don't get me wrong; this doesn't mean there are not amazing rewards and advantages that come from that discomfort and pain. There are, of course, and once we achieve our dream, we can choose to stay there, in that place of comfort—but we rarely do. Remember Kellie, who shared her story with us in "The Courage to Be Confident"? Recently she and I met again, and she shared her desire to leave her current team and take on a new one. She said, "The thing I struggle with most about this decision is that I love my team. I worked so hard to get this team going and now I'm ready to leave it. What am I thinking?"

It's a rhetorical question, really, for any courageous leader. When things get comfortable we are ready to grow again. We rarely stay put long, and rarely does achieving our Big Dream come without the sacrifice of comfort. This is where the rubber meets the road, because seldom does anyone seek out pain intentionally. No one I know gets up in the morning and says, "Today I'm choosing to risk everything I have, work like a dog, and struggle for years through emotional highs and lows that will bring me to the brink of insanity, all for the chance to achieve my dreams." It just doesn't happen. And yet, this kind of hopeful enthusiasm is what fuels us through the tough times to realize our dreams.

Maria, known as Kika to her friends and family, is the chief operating officer and cofounder of Kika Enterprises, an online eBay company she started in 2005 with her husband, Ricardo. Since its inception, Kika Enterprises has become a leader in secondary-market wireless data devices, and in 2016 was named one of America's Fast Growing Private Companies by *Inc.*[3] Maria's Big Dream was to start her own business. Both of her parents were entrepreneurs, and her father was a strong proponent of self-employment. During every family vacation, he would say to her, "Imagine if you had to ask a boss for this time off!" After finishing college, she realized her ultimate goal was to build something that would give her family the same kind of flexibility she had experienced throughout her childhood. Eleven years later, Maria, her husband, and their two young children are enjoying the lifestyle achieving her Big Dream affords her.

Not every Big Dream is the dream of entrepreneurship. For others, the Big Dream is to lead a division or a successful team, or maybe it's to be a stay-at-home parent. Possibly even to retire early, like Jack. Jack was the president and CEO of a private company, which he led through good times and bad for more than 20 years. When he was ready to retire, he sent this memo to his organization.

> It is with mixed emotions that I am announcing my retirement. I informed the Board of Directors earlier this year that I intended to transition to retirement by the end of 2016. With the support of the Board, a search for a successor was initiated immediately. Although I am still young, I want to share with you that both my parents passed away relatively young. Because of their loss, I have had a long-term goal to retire while I am healthy and capable of enjoying hobbies, like fishing, boating, and skiing, for many years to come.

After I congratulated Jack on living his Big Dream, he shared that he has many projects slated for retirement. His first is to build a wine cellar in his home. If you ask me, Jack is demonstrating just as impressive an ability to dream Big Dreams in retirement as he did in leadership.

What are your Big Dreams?

What do you want to be? What do you want to be known for? What do you want to have? What do you want to give? What about your Big Dream? How would you describe it? What does it look like, feel like, and sound like? How will you know you've achieved it? Most important, if you were to accomplish it, what is the impact to your business and the organization you lead? To your family?

Big Moves

Once we are clear about what we want to accomplish, we need to devise a plan that gets us from point A to point B. But here's the thing. We are not talking about small moves, a series of minor steps that take us only incrementally forward. When you dream big, you also have to make Big Moves, one major step forward followed by another gigantic step, and then another, and then another. Remember the 40 percent rule here.[4] You have much more in your reserves than you think. If you are clear about what you want, you have what it takes to make it happen. You just have to do it.

So what exactly characterizes a Big Move? Think about it this way: A Big Move is what propels us toward our goal faster and stronger than any other step we could take. If you want to be a real estate broker, then nothing will propel you forward faster than getting your real estate license. If you have your license, nothing will propel you forward faster than beginning marketing and networking yourself in your city. If you are a real estate broker who wants to be even more successful, nothing propels you forward more than developing your own niche within your city.

Of course, Big Moves require courage. A wonderful benefit of a Big Move is that it usually creates momentum and triggers another Big Move and then another, until Big Moves are happening so often that you find yourself moving toward your goal almost effortlessly. For example, starting my business when I was six months pregnant was a Big Move, but even bigger than that was starting a second business by leveraging the success of my first business. The result of those Big Moves then led to a relationship with John Wiley & Sons publishing company that led to an e-mail from one of its editors requesting that I consider writing a book. Without the first two Big Moves, the Big Move to write this book may not have happened at all, because the first two moves provided a significant portion of the expertise and experience needed to write this book. Who knows where the Big Move of publishing this book will lead. But I'm confident something else big will follow, allowing me to continue on the path toward achieving my Big Dreams.

Expect Success

I distinctly remember the first time I disappointed someone who expected greatness from me. That someone was my first-grade teacher. My crime was an unorganized desk, with crumpled-up papers jammed between my books. After I pulled out an assignment—wrinkled and beaten up—she yelled at me, dumped over my desk, and announced to the class that I was a mess. Seeing me in the hallway with my eyes full of tears and my head hung low, a few other faculty members were astonished to discover I was being punished. More commonly known for being the teacher's pet, rather than the troublemaker, I cried in embarrassment.

I'm 41 years old and I can still recall, as if it were yesterday, my angry teacher's ice-cold blue eyes and red pursed lips as she shouted at me. I also remember thinking, "What is it about this situation that makes her this angry?" Even a six-year-old could see her response seemed a little over the top. To be sure, it was a defining moment for me—but, luckily, in a good way. I decided I was okay with making a mess, but that did not make *me* a mess. I was the kid whom teachers loved. I wasn't going to let one incident of getting on someone's bad side change that. This failure was something I could live with. My teacher's expectations were not the ones that mattered most to me; what counted were the expectations I had of myself.

In the best seller *Performing Under Pressure: The Science of Doing Your Best When It Matters Most*, authors Hendrie Weisinger and J. P. Pawliw-Fry discuss a new way of looking at and understanding the importance of our expectations. Citing research by Dr. Marcel Kinsbourne, a neuroscientist at the New School for Social Research in New York, the authors describe an inside-out chemistry that occurs in our bodies based on our expectations. In short, Kinsbourne found that what our brain believes about a given situation has an impact on the outcome.[5]

Weisinger and Pawliw-Fry also reference multiple examples of the placebo effect, where people get the result they expect without any real medical intervention or biological explanation. For example, a study in Japan of people who were extremely allergic to poison ivy was conducted, during which the placebo effect was studied. The leaf of an innocuous plant was rubbed on one arm of each participant;

however, they were all told it was poison ivy. Researchers then rubbed a poison ivy leaf on the other arm and told participants that leaf was harmless. All 13 people in the study developed a rash where the "harmless" leaf contacted their skin, while only two experienced reactions to the real poison ivy leaves.[6]

For me, the most fascinating research I found related to this topic was conducted by the Cleveland Clinic Foundation. Researchers from multiple disciplines partnered to see whether mental power could improve muscle power. One group of participants was asked to practice mental exercises of specific fine motor skills (mentally rehearsing the exercise without any movement), while another group physically practiced the same fine motor skills. The group that mentally practiced fine motor skills increased their strength by 35 percent, and the group that practiced using physical exercise increased by 53 percent. The control group that did neither did not increase their strength at all. The researchers concluded that mental exercise does lead to increased muscular strength.[7]

What does this mean for us on our path of courageous leadership? Simply this: *The expectations we have of ourselves and the results we get are invariably similar things.*

We all have a six-year-old in us, ready to exceed everyone's expectations. As we embark on our journey toward achieving our Big Dreams, we must call on that innocence and enthusiasm and know—comfortably and without hesitation—we set our own expectations. Not a teacher, not a spouse, not a boss, not a friend. Decide what success looks like to you and expect it, and you will achieve it.

Plan for the Worst

During college, I took advantage of student loans, which covered all of my major costs, and on weekends, I drove home to work at the same restaurant job I had in high school. Halfway through my senior year, the university sent me a notice indicating I owed it $2,000, apparently the result of not qualifying for enough in loans because of a change in my family's financial situation. The letter clearly stated I would not be allowed to continue my studies until the balance was paid in full. My solution to this problem included working double shifts and as many overtime hours as possible during the holiday break, but based on my calculations, I would still be $800 short of my goal.

I explained the situation to my dad, whose response was "Well, if you want to go back to school badly enough, you'll figure out another plan." I knew he wouldn't just give me the money unless I did everything I could to make up the difference, but I did assume that my dad, who so greatly values education, would help keep me in school.

That was a really bad assumption. A few days before heading back to school, I showed him my bank account statement, proving that I had exceeded my anticipated earnings and revealing, as expected, that I was still a little short. Without hesitation he said, "Well, I guess you didn't want it bad enough, or you just didn't plan well." That was the end of the discussion.

My father didn't leave me with nothing, though. He left me with a critical lesson: You can't rely solely on plan A, even when all indicators are pointing in the right direction. Nothing is a given. That's why plan B is so vitally important. Knowing what your backup plan is—how you'll make things happen when everything you thought you could count on has fallen apart—is crucial. As you are building and evaluating your execution plan, you also need to consider all the potential cracks in the foundation. Make a list of potential oversights, pitfalls, and obstacles, and plan how you will prevent, work around, or mitigate the leaks.

Martin Seligman, a popular and well-regarded psychologist, provides some additional insight into how to plan for the unexpected in his book *Flourish*.[8] He suggests that, to deal with the worst-case scenarios, we should train for the worst-case scenarios. Seligman uses the example of snipers on the battlefield to make his point. Snipers usually endure almost two days without sleep before they locate their target and are ready to take a shot. This is the reality of the job, and yet being really good at shooting difficult targets while sleep deprived can be exceedingly difficult. Rather than trying to change the circumstances, which are likely unavoidable, or attempting to keep them awake with medication, the U.S. Army trains snipers by simulating real experiences. During training, soldiers are kept awake for two days, after which they practice making accurate shots. It is because they are placed in these harsh, real-life conditions that they get good at dealing with the tough stuff required of them on the battlefield.

To do what Seligman is suggesting requires putting yourself in situations where you will be confronted with the worst-case scenario, allowing you to practice, practice, and practice! It may sound peculiar, but during some of the most challenging times in my life, I have found myself grateful for the opportunity to learn and practice. Grateful, though not necessarily happy about it. *Gratitude* is typically not a word most people use when describing their experiences of worst-case scenarios. However, if we've planned for it and practiced our response to it, there are usually no surprises, and we are prepared for whatever it will dish up.

Build Your Board of Directors

Not long ago, I led a board of directors evaluation process for one of my clients. To assess their performance accurately, I began by talking with the multiple executives who reported to the board. I asked them many questions about their experiences with the board, from compliance and oversight to direction and support. What I heard overwhelmingly from these leaders is how significant and impactful the board was in shaping, supporting, and guiding their strategy and execution. One leader said, "I leave with nuggets of wisdom that translate to hundreds of thousands of dollars to my business."

They shared how valuable it was to have the board look in from the outside to provide an educated, independent perspective based on their veteran expertise while being independent of their organization. One surprising discovery was that these executives really enjoyed having a team dedicated to holding them accountable. Whether they realized it before the evaluation or not, they learned during the process that they were desperately seeking this kind of answerability.

Even more remarkable to me was the fact that this board met only four times a year and allocated 45 to 60 minutes to each executive during each of the quarterly meetings. Clearly, it wasn't the amount of time invested in an individual's strategy and execution that was impactful. As a matter of fact, the executives themselves said they preferred the efficiency of this interaction. It was, instead, the board's purposeful and focused effort to guide and support them that really made a difference.

Like the executives I interviewed, when you are ready to make your Big Moves to achieve your Big Dreams, who better to help you stay on track and accountable than a board of directors? You may not have a dedicated team of experts at your disposal, but you likely have a handful of people who are committed to your success, people whom you can learn from and who are willing to hold you accountable.

Yuly is a friend and colleague who immigrated to the United States from Venezuela in 2007. She is a fashion, vocation, and fitness blogger who focuses on assisting modern women in addressing all areas of their lives. When she started her blog, *Yuly360*, a mentor, her husband, and a group of women friends made up her board of directors. Not surprisingly, because she was a start-up company, she couldn't pay them a stipend for their time, but they were still committed to her success nonetheless. To ensure she had translated her material into English appropriately, her husband spent countless hours in the evenings reviewing Yuly's articles before she posted them. Her group of women friends met regularly at a nearby restaurant to talk about what was new for them as leaders and how they could best support one another. Yuly describes her board of directors as a source of inspiration and guidance, "a group of diverse trusted advisors who help shape the strategic direction of *Yuly360* for near-term and long-range business decisions." These individuals keep *Yuly360* on track and moving forward.

Recalibrating

Not long ago, while having dinner with a client and friend, he asked me a really pointed question about dreams.

> Angela, when you reach your goals (i.e., your Big Dream) how do you know that was the goal you should be shooting for? I mean, what if what you achieved was the goal, but maybe the goal should have been something else? How do you know you've picked the right goal?

The question reminded me of an activity in the Personify Leadership program. Participants are asked to establish a team goal; specifically they decide how many items they want to get through the delivery system and to the customer. We also ask them to determine their quality standard. How many errors do they consider acceptable in terms of success? After some debate among team members, the group agrees on its goal. Then, as the exercise proceeds, things begin to change. We may remove individuals from the system or add new members to the team. We may change the type of items flowing through the system or the order in which the items are received. More often than not, the team will continue doing what it initially agreed to do without changing its goal or strategy, the result of which is rarely success. Every once in a while, however, a team member will stop and say, "The environment around us has changed, but we have not changed. Our goals are still the same. Should we consider revisiting our goals?" It's at this moment that the group will realize that calibration is necessary.

According to Dictionary.com, one definition of the word *calibrate* is "to make corrections in or adjust a procedure or process."[9] When new information comes in, we can ignore it and maintain our focus, or we can consider it and evaluate whether what we are learning changes how we want to achieve our dreams—or whether our dreams need to change altogether.

At the same time I was deciding to start my first business while awaiting the birth of my first child; I was also accepted into a PhD program in another state. I decided to defer my enrollment until the following fall and give myself some time to adjust to two big moves: parenting and entrepreneurship. When the next year's registration arrived, I was already pregnant with my second child. Up until that point I had fully intended to get my PhD, and I had not at all anticipated a second child. Given the new information, I had to recalibrate. Nothing was more important to me at that time than to do what I had already committed to and to do it really, really well. For me, that meant turning down the opportunity to study and focusing on being a mom and starting a business. It was actually an easy choice for me at the time and didn't feel like giving up anything at all. Recalibration usually isn't about giving up a Big Dream but rather, as life continues to unfold, reinventing or reimagining it.

Making Your Big Move

Now you have your tool kit full of frameworks and strategies to help you lead courageously no matter the challenge or situation you face. For hundreds of pages you've explored some of the highs and lows of courageous leadership through stories shared by others. It's quite likely, if this book was successful, that your perspective of courage has forever been changed. The thing about new perspective is that you will never be able to not know what you know now. For example, you know now:

1. You have a choice between action and reaction.

2. Know who you are and what you stand for.

3. You can get unstuck and move on or go deeper.

4. Humbling Experiences will find you when you are arrogant.

5. You get to vote for you.

6. The Delegation Doom Loop is futile and doesn't help you or others grow.

7. Feedback is personal and changes everything.

8. There is a time to be in the middle, and there is a time to get out.

9. Recovery is a necessary part of courage.

10. Big Dreams don't just happen; you make them happen.

In some ways, I wish this book were different. I wish that, instead of talking about accepting pain as part of the process, I could say there is no pain associated with courage. We could take the pain scale, tear it up, and throw it out. We could make pain irrelevant. Then you could toss out the entire contents of the book and continue on your merry way with a smile. Unfortunately, that's not the way it works for us human beings. We learn from the meaning we give our pain, and we transcend our current circumstances when we go *through* them, not around them.

The good news is that we are all capable of mind-blowing, transformative, really cool things. The responsibility for closing the gap between our reality and our Big Dreams lies with us, and the tools to do it, within us. It is time now to go out and practice putting your courage muscle to good use.

So, my friends, go forward and be brave. No matter what life throws at you, be the courageous leader you know you can be. And remember, you are not alone.

Chapter Application

Take a moment and consider how you would complete these sentences:

My Big Dream is:_____

To achieve my Big Dream, I will need to make the following big moves:_____

(continued)

(continued)

Questions to Consider

1. Who makes up your board of directors?
2. What support do you need from your board of directors to achieve your Big Moves?
3. What challenges do you anticipate you'll face when making your Big Dream become a reality? How can you plan for the worst to mitigate any potential surprises?
4. How will you know you've achieved the expectations you have of yourself?

Strategies to Practice

1. Once you have identified your goals, practice using the visualizing tool introduced in "The Courage to Be Confident." Each day set aside 15 minutes to practice visualizing your Big Dream. Also, visualize yourself successfully taking Big Moves to achieve your Big Dream.
2. If you do not have a board of directors, identify people in your organization and in your circle of influence who can play a role in mentoring and coaching you toward success. Oftentimes, people around us have already accomplished what we are trying to do and are honored to help us if we ask. If you are not aware of anyone in your circle to help you, look at joining networking groups, taking classes, or even asking for an executive coach to support you or join your board of directors.
3. Share your Big Dream publicly. When we vocalize our goals to others, there is an immediate sense of accountability. Use social media to post your progress, and then enjoy the support and words of encouragement you get in return.

4. Make sure to prioritize how you spend your time and money. You cannot achieve everything and certainly not all at once. If you decide you want to achieve your Big Dream, your time and money will need to be focused on achieving your goal. Don't be tempted to waver unless you feel you need to recalibrate.

Notes

1. Ali, Muhammad. Used with permission of Muhammad Ali Enterprises, LLC.

2. Kelly Services, Inc. *Kelly Global Workforce Index (KGWI): Employee Engagement and Retention*. September 2013. http://www.kellyocg.com/ uploadedFiles/7-KellyOCG/2-Knowledge/Workforce_Trends/Employee_ Engagement_and_Retention_2013_KGWI.pdf.

3. *Inc.* editors. "Inc. 5000 2016: The Full List." 2016. http://www.inc.com/ inc5000/list/2016/.

4. Itzler, Jesse. *Living with a SEAL: 31 Days Training with the Toughest Man on the Planet*. New York: Center Street, 2015.

5. Weisinger, Hendrie, and J. P. Pawliw-Fry. *Performing Under Pressure: The Science of Doing Your Best When It Matters Most*. New York: Crown Business, 2015, page 201.

6. Blakeslee, Sandra. "Placebos Prove So Powerful Even Experts Are Surprised; New Studies Explore the Brain's Triumph Over Reality." *New York Times*, October 13, 1998. http://www.nytimes.com/1998/10/13/science/placebos-prove-so-powerful-even-experts-are-surprised-new-studies-explore-brain.html.

7. Ranganathan, Vinoth K., Vlodek Siemionow, Jing Z. Liu, Vinod Sahgal, and Guang H. Yue. "From Mental Power to Muscle Power – Gaining Strength by Using the Mind." *Neuropsychologia* 42, no. 7 (2004): 944–56. doi:10.1016/j. neuropsychologia.2003.11.018.

8. Seligman, Martin E. P. *Flourish: A Visionary New Understanding of Happiness and Well-Being*. New York: Free Press, 2011.

9. Dictionary.com, s.v. "calibrate." 2002. http://www.dictionary.com/browse/ calibrate?s=t.

ACKNOWLEDGMENTS

I am grateful to a number of people for their contribution and support in creating this book, most notably Linda Williams, for her intuitive ability to download what's in my brain to a logical outline, in addition to her effortlessly work on the details. Linda, you are incredibly talented. Thank you so much for your effort on this project.

Thank you to Roxanne Esquibel for designing the graphics that bring the concepts in the book to life in a meaningful way. Rox, your contributions, not only to this book but to our work at Personify Leadership, are what make everything we do unique, well-branded, and simply beautiful. We are grateful to have you.

A special thank you to my business partner at Personify Leadership, Michelle Cummings, for supporting the creation and launch of this book.

Thank you to the hundreds of leaders that have either directly shared their stories in this book or inspired a story indirectly. It's not easy to allow others to learn from stories of success and failure alike. Your courage allows others to learn and grow.

Thank you to the pilot book club members who provided me with feedback and allowed me to give the book a "test run," including Yuly Van Brakel, Maria Davila, Jenel Harju, Amy Haworth, Randy Lapp, Mandy Fordah, Natalia Benda Celenski, Chris Huwaldt, Katie Shaver, and Rimma Polissky.

Thank you to Dr. Nate Regier, Midge LaPorte Epstein, and Larry Simkins for being willing to put your endorsements on my first book.

I have been inspired by many great authors who have dedicated their lives to the work of leadership development in one form or another, specifically William Bridges, Chip Conley, and Brené Brown, as well as Barry Oshry and Jim Collins, who generously agreed to contribute their work to this publication.

On a personal note, thank you to Nina Lund and David Prince for being my career mentors. To Diana and Jon Sebaly for their support to make my Big Dreams come true.

And to my husband, Rick, and kids, Will and Cate, for letting me write morning, noon, and night when the inspiration set in. But above all else, thank you to my husband for believing in me—even before I did.

EPILOGUE

The Courageous Leader is based on the principles of The Spine of a Leader, one of eight core competencies used in the Personify Leadership® leadership development program. To personify leadership, it takes more than any one skill or trait. It takes all you've got!

The other seven core competencies of Personify Leadership are:

The Heart of a Leader—Be a leader whose intention is to look out for the best interests of others:

- ◆ Define your intention as a leader.
- ◆ Align your intention with the best interest of your team and organization.
- ◆ Become aware of your signals and ensure they reflect your intention.

The Mind of a Leader—Be a leader who is emotionally resilient:

- ◆ Distinguish between too little, optimal, and too much stress.
- ◆ Identify associated behaviors with stress in the workplace.
- ◆ Identify what is within our control, and how we can affect change when it is necessary to do so.

The Voice of a Leader—Be a leader who sends a message that resonates with those who receive it:

- ◆ Understand and apply basic principles of the Sender and Receiver communication model.
- ◆ Discover your Dominance, Influence, Steadiness, and Conscientiousness (DiSC) style and how it influences your behavior and communication styles.

◆ Adapt your behavior and communication to accommodate those who prefer a different style.

The Ears of a Leader—Be a leader who truly listens to others:

◆ Demonstrate an understanding of the six Interruptions to Listening.
◆ Identify the underlying intentions behind interruptions.
◆ Practice confirming and clarifying listening skills to ensure that another's message has been received as intended.

The Hands of a Leader—Be a leader who provides direction and support:

◆ Identify obstacles and benefits to delegation, and learn ways to overcome the Delegation Doom Loop.
◆ Leverage delegation as a developmental process that includes a structured and well-thought-out delegation conversation.
◆ Apply the appropriate mode of delegation for the delegate, the project, and the situation.

The Feet of a Leader—Be a leader who walks the talk:

◆ Demonstrate an understanding of mirror neurons in leadership.
◆ Identify where we are choosing to be victims of the law of reciprocity rather than ending the cycle of not playing nicely.
◆ Demonstrate the ability to take personal accountability.

The Eyes of a Leader—Be a leader who has a vision of the future:

◆ Create a vision for success.
◆ Eliminate energy drains and other roadblocks to your success.
◆ Execute your vision.

To learn more about Personify Leadership, go to www.personifyleadership.com. To learn more about the author of *The Courageous Leader*, Angela Sebaly, please visit www.angelasebaly.com.

ABOUT THE AUTHOR

Angela Sebaly is cofounder and CEO of the firm Personify Leadership, a training provider. Formerly the vice president of leadership development for a global oil, gas, and chemicals inspection company, Angela also serves as principal consultant for the firm Invested Leadership, an Executive Coaching firm. An entrepreneur developing a global presence, Angela has been coaching, facilitating, and leading teams and organizations for over two decades. Education, communication, and courage are the pillars of her life's work. She lives with her family in Fort Lauderdale.

INDEX

Page references followed by *fig* indicate an illustrated figure; followed by *t* indicates a table.

for receiving feedback well in the,
138–142; Lucas's story on having
confidence in the, 92–93; recovery
in the, 171–179. *See also* Culture;
Environment; Organizations
Worst-case scenarios: having gratitude for
learning from, 189; planning for,
188–189